GOD
Laughs

40 Days of
Humour & Devotion

REED FLEMING

WESTBOW
PRESS®
A DIVISION OF THOMAS NELSON
& ZONDERVAN

WestBow Press books may be ordered through booksellers or by contacting:

WestBow Press
A Division of Thomas Nelson & Zondervan
1663 Liberty Drive
Bloomington, IN 47403
www.westbowpress.com
844-714-3454

Unless otherwise noted, All Scripture quotations are taken from the Holy Bible,
NEW INTERNATIONAL VERSION®, NIV® Copyright © 1973, 1978,
1984, 2011 by Biblica, Inc.® Used by permission. All rights reserved worldwide.

Scripture quotation marked (KJV) taken from King
James version of the Bible, public domain.

ISBN: 979-8-3850-4003-2 (sc)
ISBN: 979-8-3850-4004-9 (e)

Print information available on the last page.

WestBow Press rev. date: 01/24/2024

CONTENTS

ACKNOWLEDGEMENTS AND THANKS

Thanks to my boon companion, God the Father, Son, and Holy Spirit,

I want to thank Linda, my greatest cheerleader and proofreader and our grown children David and Judith. You supply all the love a guy could want and oh so many sermon illustrations.

I also want to thank the Rev. Geoff de Jong for his help in proofreading and editing.

Joy Alloway has long been a wonder of encouragement.

The folks of Threshold Ministries have been a supportive family for these many years.

Last but certainly not least my grandsons Declan and Ronan. You always bring a smile to your grandpa's face.

PROLOGUE

My goal in writing is to share with readers passages in Scripture that I find amusing. I will tell or retell these stories with the hope of demonstrating their humour and practical 'life lessons' that can be drawn from them. We find things humorous which we recognize as common experiences or foibles. The biblical characters stand in for us at our most foolish. We are amused because we see our common humanity and we smile at the things which are not funny when pointed out in ourselves.

I trust that you will laugh, along with me, but also that we can learn, grow, and even repent together as the 'funny' becomes a mirror into our own lives.

DAY 1

"It is the woman you gave me!"
Genesis 3:1 - 19

DID YOU EVER WONDER WHY WE FIND THINGS FUNNY. THE comedian steps toward a banana peel. We hold our collective breath. Will he step on it? Will he 'slip' and do an embarrassing prat fall? Inevitably he does and we laugh. Why? Because slipping and falling is a part of the human experience. While I have never literally slipped on a banana peel (I actually do not know anyone who has.) I have most definitely 'slipped.' Whether it is an actual fall, a slip of the tongue or our slip was showing, it is a shared experience. Alexander Pope penned the immortal words, "to err is human" and in doing so he captured truth.

It is rarely funny, though when I am the one falling. Humour needs its distance! Anything hitting too close to home is nearer to tragedy than comedy, but, oh how funny a blooper accomplished by someone else can be! Have you ever stumbled walking down the sidewalk and stopped to stare at the pavement behind as if it conspired to trip you. In your mind you say, "It can not be my own clumsiness it must be the fault of the 'uneven' walkway!"

Blame-shifting is only a nano second younger than erring! We look around, then, to see if anyone has noticed. If we have been seen we make a demonstration of disgust with the offending pathway and collect our dignity and stride on. The loss of dignity, our and attempts to regain it, amuse us if it is not our dignity at play.

The first such 'err' set the stage for bloopers and pratfalls yet to come. Until that moment the axiom "to err is human" was not at all applicable or remotely true! The human race was in its earliest of laps when the first error was committed. God had been clear to our progenitors, "And the Lord commanded "You are free to eat from any tree in the garden; but you must not eat from the tree of the knowledge of good and evil…"." He did not explain why, for the Creator does not answer to the created. In his wisdom he simply forbade that which would bring incalculable harm to his beloved creation.

You know the rest of the story, but as an author I must needs retell it. They chose to eat the forbidden fruit, seeking equality with God! Because our forebears chose self-centred rebellion, thus setting a similar course for all of humanity, they were no longer fit for a sinless paradise such as Eden. Their choices made life in this environment untenable. This led to a separation from their Creator and the idyllic creation. They now were faced with life in a thorn riddled world and the inevitability of death. One might say that Eve was duped, that she was deceived into eating the forbidden fruit and I am sure that would be her explanation. But it is no real explanation it is but an excuse! Yes she was tempted, but it was her decision to give in. The serpent lied and cajoled and she fell for it despite the clear knowledge of God's one demand.

While Eve's excuse was lame Adam has none at all! "She gave some to her husband; and he did eat!" No trickery, no deception, no persuasion needed. Adam simply ate!

I recall getting into trouble with my little brother. We came home muddy and wet from playing by the pond, near our home. We tracked the filth into the house where I was met by an angry mother. I took the brunt of the punishment with the words "You are older! You knew better!" ringing in my ears. Adam was the senior and yet he seems to be the easiest 'mark' of the two. It is no wonder he goes down in history as the one responsible for the epic fall!

Now caught with a mouthful of forbidden fruit, very much like a toddler with his hand in the cookie jar, Adam points the finger. Perhaps better said he points the fingers, for he has multiple scapegoats! With one he points squarely at the woman, his wife! It is this woman. She is to blame. Ignoring his own autonomy and his responsible place in creation he attempts to shift the blame!

I find this so humorous because I recognize this finger pointing excuse making in me. It is comical in him because it is so real and tragic in me! Caught 'red handed' he does not hold up his hand to assume responsibility but instead so lamely tries to deflect blame. No reasonable adult (or child) would fail to see through his poor defenses, and yet by reflex he foolishly attempts to shift responsibility.

Even Adam in all his naivety must have realized that pointing at the woman was not going to fully absolve him, he next resorted to pointing to God. Have you ever noticed that when things go well we easily pat ourselves on the back, but when trouble comes, we are much more likely to lay the blame at God's door?

It is not just the woman, but it is "the woman you gave me!" How could God have acted in such folly as to create this creature that would bring him so low? His twisted logic seeks to absolve himself and to blame God. In the sin but also in the excuse making Adam paved the way for humanity as we now experience it. The all-knowing God does not even consider the feeble excuse making then, nor does He today!

Our efforts to avoid responsibility by pointing fingers must seem ludicrous to the omniscient (all knowing) God. How often am I the unwitting comedy in my own tragedy?

I have not yet described the dire consequences of this 'humorous' exchange, because the comedy get seriously unfunny quickly. Innocence is squandered! The Fall is far, and universal! While we smile at the comedy, comedy itself is a by product of this great loss. I cannot imagine what was laughable before but now we laugh at our own expense. H.L. Menken is credited with saying, "When you point a finger there are three pointing back at you" and it rings of truth. This is, perhaps, why Jesus warns against judging, lest we be judged!

I find this inept excuse making by Adam really quite amusing until I recognize that I share this feeble trait as surely as I share in his Fall. Paul pens in Romans 3:23 "For all have sinned and fall short...." We are all in need of a Saviour. I am so glad that I have one! Because Jesus rescued me I can laugh at my frailties knowing that Jesus has paid the consequences so I can be freed and forgiven.

The serpent thought he had won but, God gets the last laugh! Playwright and poet John Heywood wrote "He who laughs last, laughs best!," and I think he was surely right!

DAY 2

JONAH AND THE WORM JONAH 3 & 4 ONE OF THE LEAST TOLD stories from scripture is Jonah and.... (no not that creature) the worm. In this tale Jonah demonstrates an amusing pettiness which reminds me of my own.

The reader is likely familiar with the context. Jonah has been instructed by God to go to the city of Ninevah and deliver a message for them to repent. Our intrepid hero then sets off in the entirely different direction. Well might we ask, "Why did he do that?." A little background information is helpful at this point. Nineveh was the great city of the Assyrian Empire. We might understand the Assyrians by comparing them to the 'Wild Bunch' a motorcycle gang mercilessly terrorizing a quiet community. The Assyrians had a long history with Israel! It was a history of pillage and carnage. In fact, the ten tribes which formed the Northern Kingdom, Israel, was taken into captivity ending its existence as a distinct nation.

To say that Jonah did not care for Nineveh or its inhabitants would be the grossest of understatements! It was his hatred of Assyria that caused Jonah to rebel against God's calling on his life. You may be excused for thinking that my humorous tale would be of his sojourn in the gastric section of a great fish before being belched on shore outside Nineveh, but that may be a story for another day.

Reeking of fish and perhaps bleached blond in the digestive juices and fish guts, he does enter the great city. He proclaims God's judgement on Nineveh lest they repent. Then the thing he feared most happened. Nineveh took seriously the message! In sackcloth and ashes, they lamented their collective sin. Still Jonah had hope that God would not be merciful toward guilty humanity. He made himself a little nest on a hill overlooking the metropolis, from which he could view the destruction the Assyrians so richly deserved. As he was waiting and watching the sun beat cruelly on his crown. God graciously provided a vine to grow atop that hill and it produced shade to provide him relief so he could await Nineveh's destruction in relative comfort. While he was waiting in anticipation in the shade of that vine, God delivered another message to Jonah in the form of a worm. (It amazes us how slow Jonah was to learn about the mercy and grace of God until we look closely at our own hearts.) This worm devoured Jonah's vine! He sat on the hilltop in the blazing Middle East sunshine fuming at God about the destruction of his beloved vine.

It seems that Jonah is finally at the place to have a conversation with God. God asks, "Do you have any right to be angry?" "I do! I am angry enough to die!" (Jonah 4:9) God goes on to point out the absurdity of Jonah's anger. He is furious about a vine that grew overnight and died overnight but he has no compassion for a city of one hundred and twenty thousand souls. Scripture does not tell Jonah's response to God, but we have hope that like Job when confronted by God, he realised his folly.

One of the earliest concepts children learn is 'fairness.' I well remember a lesson from my own father in answer to a complaint that he was not acting fairly. He said, "The last thing you want in life is to be treated the way you deserve!" I must admit, like so many of my dad's lessons, I did not understand it at the time. I know now that rather than fairness; I desire mercy and grace. Mercy is 'not getting what I deserve' and grace is 'getting what I do not deserve.'

Jonah was hesitant (to say the least) to go to Nineveh because God was likely to show mercy. He knew they did not deserve mercy. They richly deserved retribution for all they had done! Though he was a recipient of mercy repeatedly he did not want it extended to others. He was a man of mercurial temperament which may be why I am drawn to him. He demonstrates my unwillingness to extend to others the mercy I desperately crave for myself. He illustrates the tendency to accept vine-like grace and take it for granted as if deserved.

Jonah is a story of high comedy and low belief. In Jonah we recognize ourselves. We can laugh at this sunburned, fish stinking, prophet but as we do so, can we recognize and repent of our own hypocrisy ? The folks of Nineveh managed to repent, Should we do less? Repent does not just mean feeling sorry. It means to turn around, to change our attitudes and behaviours and bring them in line with God's will and in line with his holiness.

DAY 3

Friend of Sinners
Luke 15:2

THERE IS A TRADITIONAL BALLAD "THE BONNY EARL OF MURRAY" which created a new word in the English language. The word is mondegreen. It means to mishear or misinterpret a spoken phrase. The original words in the ballad were "laid him on the green" but many heard "Lady Mondegreen," and so entered a new word for a common circumstance.

Children have misinterpreted Christmas carols and wondered "Who is Round John Virgin?"

I had such an incident involving scripture.

We called our parents' friends Aunt Edith and Uncle Glen. We loved going to visit them because Uncle Glen had a gas station with a pop machine, and he would give us each a soda when we called.

One Sunday as I was fidgeting in church a Bible passage being read got my attention. The passage told of Jesus being a friend of sinners and then came the arresting part "and Edith with them!" I was 'blown away' with the idea that my Aunt Edith had a personal friendship with Jesus!

In due course I learned of my mondegreen, but I also learned that Edith did indeed have a personal friendship with Jesus, and so could I. The great accusation hurled at Jesus was "The man receiveth of sinners and eateth with them." (Luke 15:2 KJV) This set him apart from all other religious leaders of his day. They sought to be holy by separating themselves from the 'unholy' lest they became contaminated. Jesus instead gladly mixed with sinners in order that he might save or decontaminate them.

It was at a celebratory dinner party that the Pharisees first uttered this complaint. Through this event we learn a couple of very important truths. Jesus came to "seek and to save the lost" (Luke 19:10). He was uniquely suited for this because of his sinless character he was not infected by the nearness to sinners, but rather because of his divine nature's touch He made sinners clean. In doing this the 'curse of the Fall' was being reversed!

Another important lesson to be drawn is that there is a special opportunity that comes when we share food and 'break bread' together. The early Church of Acts seems to recall this as they were noted for eating together. Somehow over time this example has been de-emphasized in Christian culture. The power of generous hospitality has been blunted.

These last few years I have been much encouraged by Dave and Jon Ferguson's book "BLESS" and Michael Frost's "Surprise the World." In their book BLESS the Ferguson's use bless as an acronym for creating a soul winning lifestyle. The 'E' stands for eating together with those who may not yet know Jesus. In his book Frost uses the acronym BELLS in which the 'E' stands for eating together with those who may not yet know Jesus. Both books make a convincing case that eating with 'sinners' was a strategy of Jesus for winning the 'lost,' and that the early Church followed that example. As I wrote earlier this was an accusation hurled at Jesus, by the Pharisees. It was this very kind of behaviour that led to their hatred and ultimately to the cross. I wonder sometimes how often that indictment can be lodged against me?

Perhaps taking up my cross and following him involves hosting a dinner party to which I invite, not solely my friends who know Jesus, but more importantly friends I have made who may not yet know him. I end with one last mondegreen. A child had a stuffed Teddy whose googly eyes were fixed looking at one another. He named him Gladly, in remembrance of the hymn. Perhaps you have sung it "Gladly the Cross I'd Bear." Let us pick up our cross and our guest list and get partying!

DAY 4

The Uninvited Guests
John 2: 1 -11

ANYONE WHO HAS 'BEEN EATEN OUT OF HOUSE AND HOME' BY teenagers ought to sympathize with the wedding organizers when Jesus showed up with twelve, mostly fishermen, ready to party hearty!

There was a wedding in Cana. It appears that Jesus' mother has a keen interest in this marriage feast. Jesus is invited to the party and scripture tells us he attended bringing along his twelve disciples. I live on Canada's East Coast, and I know the reputation of hard living and hard drinking fishermen. I would hate to be the recipient of a tab for an open bar as a gaggle of these bellied up! I do not know whether Jesus' friends were the direct cause of the wine well running dry, but it does not stretch imagination to assume they did their part!

In the culture of the day running out of wine was not an auspicious way to begin a successful marriage. Such an event would bring disgrace on the hosts who would be the brunt of wedding jokes for years to come. Mary comes to Jesus with the problem. She has been cherishing in her heart for the past thirty years and now acts on all that pondering. She insists that Jesus do something.

As far as she is concerned it is time for her son to begin to reveal himself. Jesus seems to demur but Mary acts in faith telling the nearby servants to do what Jesus tells them.

The result is the first sign that Jesus is the Messiah initiating the Kingdom of God!

Sitting near are six huge earthenware vessels. They were as empty as the religious rites for which they were purposed. They were set aside for the function of 'ceremonial cleansing', each held up to thirty gallons. Jesus instructed the servants to fill these with water and take it and serve the guests. This amount would be more than sufficient even for a crowd of rowdy fishermen! What good would quantity be if it were but water? When the servants poured it was no longer ordinary water it had become extraordinary wine! The servants knew its origin, but the guests only knew its excellence. That the party was saved might have been wonderful in itself, but John the Gospel writer points to this as the First Sign Jesus did. The symbolism of the wonderful new wine ought not to be lost. In these last days God has poured out His Spirit as surely as those servants decanted that new wine. Jesus begins His ministry with this wine of the wedding feast and poetically He in his Last Supper He institutes the sharing of wine in remembrance of His death until His coming again. In fact, He tells us that He will not drink again of the wine until the Marriage Supper of the lamb and His Bride the Church. The thirsty uninvited guest may amuse us, but the Bride Groom of Heaven amazes us!

He comes to take our ordinary lives, destined for judgement, and make them extraordinary and eternal. He says, "I have come that they may have life, life to the full."

In the days of Jesus' earthly walk it was traditional to serve the best wine first. Like the wedding guests though we learn that God is saving the best for the last!

DAY 5

In the Spring of the Year
2 Samuel 11

TENNYSON WROTE "IN THE SPRING A YOUNG MAN'S FANCY TURNS to thoughts of love." The young man's thoughts probably drifted there in order not to have to think about all the grueling work that springtime portends.

It was the spring of the year. It was the time of preparation of my mother's huge garden for planting. It was the spring of the year and … I hopped on my bike and headed out to hang out with my friends! My mother was not much amused!

King David had a moment early in his rule. "In the spring of the year when the kings go out to war David … sent Joab"! His thoughts turned to idleness. As King he did not have to hop a bike or chariot to avoid his duty. No one was 'the boss' of him.

This one line about David has long brought a smile to my face. This sentence like so many jokes and puns has an unexpected ending. We expect to read "In the spring of the year when kings go out to war, David led the armies of Israel." The unexpected non-sequitur stops my attention and tickles my 'funny bone.' The story like so many quickly turns serious and then tragic. The irony is that David would have been safer in the heat of battle than on his cool rooftop! The story goes on to describe him one evening getting out of bed. While Joab and his men are occupied in the nation's business, David has been lounging in bed and now arises and ascends his rooftop. Today he would have likely begun to scroll on his phone. While on the roof he catches a glimpse of a woman bathing. He then choses to leer; noting her beauty. The flame of lust is lit in him and goes unchecked leading to adultery, rape, and ultimately to murder. With each step David moves further and further into sin. What began as shirking his responsibilities to man and God, became a steep slippery slope. I am sure he never imagined the consequences for himself, his family, the nation nor did he reflect on God and His glory!

I believe the saying "Watch out for that first step, it's a doozy." originated with that great philosopher Bugs Bunny. David's first step of indolence turned out to be a doozy, indeed!

As the story progresses the funny line I enjoy so much leads on to dramatically unfunny results. Many years later, Solomon (David's son) in Proverbs, perhaps reflecting on his father's sin, writes "There is a way that seems right to a man, but in the end it leads to death."

Will I learn from this heartbreaking tale, which is recorded "for instruction in righteousness"? When I am tempted to a relatively small sin can I pause and imagine for a moment what the end might be? I laugh at the line regarding King David and the spring of the year because I recognize that same rebellious selfishness in me. I can enjoy the irony and mirth, but I ought to shun the urge to such rebellion. There is no good at the end of that way. It leads to death.

I am grateful that Jesus, though He was righteous, became sin so I could be made right! I have no hope apart from the cross of Christ. I can also rely on the Helper, the Holy Spirit to empower me to turn from temptation and walk in a manner worthy of so great a salvation!

DAY 6

Hoist on His Own Petard The Book of Esther

AS AN ADOLESCENT I FOUND THE PHRASE "HOIST ON HIS OWN petard" quite amusing, even more so when I learned that petard had a double meaning, one of which was to pass gas. What adolescent boy does not find flatulence a source of rich humour?

The phrase originates from Shakespeare's Hamlet and like many of his phrases this has been adopted as a modern-day colloquialism. Hoist means 'to lift up or raise' (a banner being hoisted into the rafters), and a petard was a bomblet, usually used to breach a locked door or gate. Hamlet's phrase then uses the image of the bomb intended for one's enemies instead blowing up in one's own face. Just thinking about this conjures up pictures of Wile E. Coyote blowing himself up while the Road Runner beep beeps off merrily. The word 'petard' (bomblet) was also used to describe the similar sounds of passing gas.

Beside laughing at bodily function noises, I also had a penchant for what may be called 'gallows humour' which is using bending toward humour rather than giving in to despair. There was no shortage of challenging times in life, and we can either laugh or cry. In my family everything was fodder for laughter. Today's story combines the irony of petard hoisting and gallows humour, and so falls right in my 'funny bone' wheelhouse.

The anti-hero of our story, Haman, is hoist on a petard of his own making but rather than a bomblet it was a gallows of his own making. Haman is a man of some influence in the Persian empire. He is described as an Agagite which means he is an Amalekite descended from King Agag. Agag many years earlier was conquered by King Saul and though Saul was instructed to kill him, Agag was spared. (Petards remind us that past mistakes can come back to haunt us.)

Haman seems a textbook case of a malignant narcissist. He feels that Mordecai, the Jew, has not shown the proper deference to him and purposes in his black heart to exact revenge. He uses his influence in the palace court to enact a plot to not only kill Mordecai, but the whole Jewish race. He is so confident in his plans that he literally built a gallows on which he plans to hoist Mordecai.

Unknown to Haman, a young Jewish woman, Esther, has risen to a place of influence in empire, as well. Mordecai points out to his young relative, Esther, that God may have placed her in this situation "for such a time as this." Esther risks her royal standing and indeed her very life and uncovers Haman's evil plan to the King. The King rises up in ager and demands the execution of Haman and he is hoisted on the very gallows he had built for Mordecai, while Mordecai is exalted to the position of influence once enjoyed by our story's villain.

Today in Jewish homes as this story is retold, the children boo at every mention of Haman. He is a picture of evil being conquered and good ultimately triumphing.

As Jesus was hoisted up on the cross the Devil seemed to have won the day, but Satan is hoist on his own petard! The death which seemed to defeat Christ's claims, ended in resurrection and triumph! The ultimate malignant narcissist is defeated by his own instrument, in this case the cross of Jesus. Like the proverbial 'petard' his stench may linger but his end is sure! Let us rejoice!

DAY 7

Sheep?
Psalm 100:3

THERE ARE SO MANY EXAMPLES OF GOD CALLING US SHEEP THAT it is hard to pick one. David, himself a noted shepherd, gives us several. In Psalm 100 he writes "We are His people, the sheep of His pasture." In Matthew 25, Jesus, the self-identified 'Good Shepherd,' speaks about separating the sheep from the goats. From the Kingdom view it is much preferable to be a sheep though this world's view differs substantially.

Ask someone who has experience with sheep, and almost immediately we hear "Sheep are not the most intelligent of creatures!" We could go on to learn that they are also tasty and easily fleeced. Jesus calls the horrid character Herod "that old fox" but calls us His sheep. Teenage me would much prefer to be the goat or the fox. Both suggest an independence and self-reliance. In those days, the idea of voluntarily identifying as a sheep seemed ludicrous to me!

Apparently, though, God does not give teenage boys a vote on this. If we are followers of the Good Shepherd then we are necessarily sheep. As I said earlier sheep are not known for their wisdom. Owl would be creatures that exemplify that, but we are not called to be owls! Foxes are noted for slyness, but fox-likeness is clearly not recommended. Sheep rely on the wisdom of the shepherd.

It seems that most animals have some sort of defence. Sharp teeth, agility, colouration, hideous taste, smell, quills, flight, or speed protect them, but the lamb has none of these. The only protection for the sheep is the shepherd and the most dangerous place for a sheep is astray from that shepherd. Earlier I spoke. about how easily fleeced the sheep are. Deception has long been a chief tool of our enemy the devil, who is like a roaring lion seeking to devour. Some time ago I learned that the first symptom that I am being deceived is …. that I do not know it! I am particularly prone to deception and can be completely oblivious to it, and as someone who can be so easily duped, I am in dire need of a wise Shepherd to guide me "along right paths." As a sheep has no defence from the roaring lion except for the shepherd so I am reliant on the Good shepherd to protect me. It does lie with me to stay close to the Shepherd and to listen for and heed his voice. At first blush this seems confining (and outwardly it is) but is God's means of leading us to abundant living and green pastures beside still waters.

The thought of being an easily fleeced helpless sheep would be comical but for the fact that Jesus is not just the Good Shepherd, he is also the Lamb of God who takes away the sin of the world. Though tempted in all ways like us he was not duped. "…like a lamb led to the slaughter and a sheep before its shearers is silent, so He did not open his mouth." (Isaiah 53:7) What a contrast our Shepherd is to us!

"We all like sheep, have gone astray, each has turned to our own way; and the LORD has laid on Him the iniquity of us all." (Isaiah 53: 6) Jesus plays a dual role in God's redemptive purposes as both the Great High Priest offering the sacrifice and at the same time as the sacrificial Lamb of God.

It is certainly a humble thing to identify as a sheep but in such humility I find safety, security and the everlasting love and care of the Great Shepherd of the sheep, King Jesus.

DAY 8

Mirror Mirror!
Romans 12:3

THE HUMAN CAPACITY FOR SELF-DELUSION IS A SOURCE OF continuing amusement. Singer Kenny Rogers sang a song "The Greatest" about a little boy proclaiming he was indeed the greatest batter ever. He tossed up the ball and took a mighty swing. Swish, he missed. Strike one! Undaunted he uttered the same self-confident refrain. Swish, once more! Strike two! Again, he proclaims his greatness and with an even greater swing ... Strike three! We expect him to lose assurance in the face of his failure but undaunted he proclaims himself

"The greatest pitcher ever!"

A survey was conducted amongst students on a university campus. They were asked to grade themselves on their appearance. Ninety percent said they were 'above average looking.' Either the surrounding population was exceptionally hideous or, more likely, they had an inflated idea of their own appearance. Paul writes "Do not think of yourself more highly than you ought, but rather think of yourself with sober judgement." (Romans 12:3)

Much humour is derived from displays of this lack of self-awareness. In the family I grew up in we delighted to catch each other in such inconsistency, but we never enjoyed our turn as the brunt of the joke. We learned an expression which encapsulated this experience, "It's no fun being Herman!"

What is funny in others cuts too close to 'the bone' for me!

James has some fun with this penchant toward self-delusion, "Do not merely listen to the word, and so deceive yourselves. Do what it says. Anyone who listens to the word but does not do what it says is like someone who looks at his face in the mirror, and after looking at himself, goes away and immediately forgets what he looks like." (James 1:22-23)

It is easy to delude ourselves into thinking we are 'Christ followers' because we attend church or read our Bible, but James, here, warns us that we fall comically short of real true faith in so doing. The world points fingers and laughs at Christian who are un-Christlike. Like most comedy played out to its final outcome, we end not in peals of laughter but in tragedy. God is not honoured by deluded Christians who claim the status but do not do the works. "Not everyone who says 'Lord, Lord,' shall enter the Kingdom of Heaven, but only the one who does the will of my Father who is in Heaven." (Matthew 7:21)

The World is not won by the comic witness of the self-righteous but by honest testimony, as C. H. Spurgeon said, "One beggar telling another beggar where to find bread." Let us learn to laugh at ourselves and in utmost honesty recommend our Redeemer to a world, which like us, needs a Saviour. Revelation 12: 11 reminds us that we triumph by the blood of the Lamb and by word of our testimony.

DAY 9

Jesus Heals a Mother-in-law
Mark 1:30 - 31

MY TEACHERS WOULD ACCUSE ME OF BEING 'THE CLASS CLOWN' and though they did not mean it this way, I took this as a compliment. I loved to make people laugh. I loved the great comedians of that age: Milton Berle, Bob Hope, Henny Youngman, Rodney Dangerfield, and George Gobel. One of their regular targets for humour was 'mothers-in-law.' It seemed each was burdened with a mother-in-law who did not appreciate them. As I grew up I learned that humour that picked on others was the lowest form of comedy, but I have maintained a perverse pleasure in mother-in-law jokes. Because I was young I, of course, had no mother-in-law. They were like mythical creatures. I assumed that mothers-in-law trooped onto the ark with every other creature. I think this remoteness from real human mothers-in law made these jokes continuously funny to me.

Lonesome George Gobel once admitted "I have not talked to my mother-in-law for eighteen months. I hate to interrupt her!" It was a real comedy downer for me that when I married I inherited perhaps the sweetest mother-in-law in the known world! It was galling that I could never honestly opine about my mother-in-law. I was robbed of a deep lode of humour material.

I say all this because my one enduring mother-in-law joke involves Jesus. Early in his career as healing Rabbi and Messiah he visited Peter's house. It was a major coup for Peter. It is not every day that the Messiah drops by for a nosh! The whole town will soon be beating its way to Peter's door with all the sick and lame and blind, but there is one fly in the ointment. There is one 'wet blanket' on the festivities. It is, of course, Peter's mother-in-law! She was sick in bed with a fever and a raucous revival meeting would disturb her recovery. Here Jesus demonstrates an unmatched level of compassion. He would go on to touch lepers and raised the dead, but here he sets the bar sky high. He heals a mother-in-law. His compassion credentials are forever sealed with this superlative act of kind-heartedness. Peter's mother-in-law gets up and against type begins to serve them all. If Jesus would condescend to reach a mother-in-law, there could be no one beyond his loving touch!

If unlike me, you find nothing funny about mothers-in-law, perhaps you can cite other biblical examples of Jesus' compassion that become for you emblems of his character and assurances that we are within the scope of his redeeming touch. He calls out to the Father to forgive those who crucify him. He gladly welcomes the thief on the adjacent cross, who moments before had mocked him. He restored Peter the denier. He even met personally with Paul the persecutor on his way to Damascus!

His love and forgiveness are among his most compelling traits. It is this love that calls us to come and follow after him. It is this compassion that spurs us on to acts of compassion ourselves. Even if that involves loving and blessing our mother-in-law!

Perhaps one day I will be half so sweet as my mother-in-law. (Do not hold your breath!)

DAY 10

Peter and the Oxymoron
Matthew 16:16 - 23

I COLLECT OXYMORONS. I STARTED JUST BECAUSE THE WORD 'oxymoron' struck me as an amusing term. An oxymoron is a figure of speech which is or appears to be self-contradictory. Some of my favourites are jumbo shrimp, only option, original copy, seriously funny, small crowd. Comedian George Carlin added: business ethics and military intelligence. An addition in recent times is fake news.

The capacity that humans have for self-contradiction is staggering and highly amusing. Inconsistency seems to be one of the few constants in human behaviour. The late-night television monologues delight in directing attention to this aspect in today's newsmakers, and we laugh. Like much humour it can become unfunny the moment the spotlight turns to our inconsistency.

Perhaps the greatest Biblical example of an oxymoron is given to us by Peter. Today's story is a splendid example Peter has a wonderful capacity to 'put his foot in his mouth' and as usual he does so spectacularly. Jesus has taken his disciples on a retreat to Caesaria Phillipi. There He asks this inner group "Who do people say that I am?." The replies come thick and fast; "John the Baptist," Jeremiah," "Elijah." Jesus then asks, "Who do you say that I am?" I imagine this is followed by an awkward silence as those gathered take in the import of this question and its answer. Peter as usual is the first to break the silence. He blurts out the immortal words "You are the Messiah, the Son of the living God." (Matthew 16:16) Here for the first time in human history is the confession of Jesus nature and saving role! This is Peter at his absolute best! Jesus commends him for being in tune with the Spirit. "Blessed are you, Simon son of Jonah, for this was not revealed to you by flesh and blood, but by my Father in heaven." (Matthew 16:17) Jesus goes on to teach that on the basis of this, Peter's confession, He would build his triumphant church! The moment is so fraught with impact that Jesus marks it by changing Peter's name from Simon to Peter, meaning rock. Every time from then on as he was called by the name Peter, he would recall the pinnacle that was this confession! I hope he enjoyed that wonderful moment because it was short-lived. As the story proceeds he will once again 'put his foot in it.'

From the time of this revelation that Jesus was come as the Messiah and the Son of God, Jesus began sharing the means by which he would redeem his people. For the first time he explained to his disciples that He would go to Jerusalem and suffer and be killed. (Matthew 16:21). The disciples like all Israel were expecting a much different Messiah. They looked for a political leader who would establish a 'Golden Age' for Israel. Perhaps these followers of his had even imagined the cabinet positions they might hold in this coming kingdom. The idea of suffering Messiah, though prophesied by Isaiah, was alien to them and their thinking.

The freshly named Peter, in the afterglow of 'his moment' steps forward to straighten Jesus out, and in doing so utters the ultimate example of an oxymoron. He says, "Never Lord!" In those words, he essentially says "No Lord!" These words are self-contradictory. Either the 'No!' is true and the 'Lord' is false, or the 'Lord' is true and the 'No!' is not!

If Jesus is Lord then our response can never be "Never!" The famous missionary Hudson Taylor said "Christ is either Lord of all or is not Lord at all." There is no room for Peter's response. Jesus takes no time to put Peter's reaction in its proper place. "Get behind me Satan!" Peter went from conduit of the Holy Spirit to dupe of Satan in record time!

Peter so often brings me amusement until I 'look in a mirror' and see myself in this impetuous saint. I am reminded that my constant disposition is to be "Yes Lord" and that any other reaction deserves a comeuppance similar to Peter's. My computer has some default settings. Occasionally I want a different font or margin and I have to make the necessary changes, but next time I open the program it reverts back to the default (did you catch the oxymoron in that?). Likewise, I should have as a default setting "Yes Lord."

It is a good thing to learn from our own mistakes, but it is an even better thing to learn from the errors of others. Let us take a lesson from Peter's ultimate oxymoron and live lives of ready obedience to the will of the one we acknowledge as Lord.

DAY 11

The Emperor's Wardrobe
Ephesians 6

ONE OF THE ENDURING AND ENDEARING STORIES IS THAT OF HANS Christian Andersen, "The Emperor's New Clothes." The story particularly amuses young readers as it exposes adult prideful blindness.

In the story two con men pretend to be the finest of tailors. They assure the Emperor that they have discovered a beautiful fabric that can only be seen and appreciated by those who are wise. They proceed to pretend to fashion a garment for His Highness. None of the people of the court want to admit that they cannot see this exotic material and so proclaim it as all together lovely! The Emperor himself is also too embarrassed to admit that he cannot see the material and acts as if he can see this fabulous robe. He arranges to parade around the streets of the city in order to show off the fine attire.

Everyone gushes over the new clothes until a child pipes up "The Emperor is not wearing anything!" That little one's honesty opened the floodgates until everyone acknowledged that indeed the Emperor had no clothes. This humorous story points to the ease with which we can be deluded and the pride which so easily leads to a fall.

Scripture tells us that we are to "put on Christ" (Romans 13:14). Elsewhere we read "Put on the full Armour of God." (Ephesians 6:11) I wonder, though, how often we like the Emperor parade around as if we have donned this essential Christian apparel? Paul writes to Timothy about such people, "having a form of godliness but denying its power." (2Timothy 3:5)

When I was a teenager there was a fad called "streaking." This involved running, usually through a crowd, with no clothes on. I propose that there are many "Spiritual Streakers," people who have perhaps plunked on a Helmet of Salvation but have never progressed in putting on the full armour. Unlike Andersen's story which amuses us, the tale of our own spiritual state of undress ought to cause us to rethink our condition and return to God, for this is the very essence of repentance.

I am convinced that if we are consciously clad in Christ, that we will we act like Him and attract others to the faith that is transforming us. This may not be the fashion of the World and its culture but in God's eyes this is the height of style.

DAY 12

Elisha and the Bears
2 Kings 2:23 - 25

I LIKE IT WHEN HEROES FROM THE BIBLE ACT IN HUMAN AND relatable ways. I especially enjoy it when there are flashes of anger. Anger has long been a near companion to me. I deal daily with the fallout of PTSD and anger is a split second away at any moment. I love to see these biblical characters express anger. There are very few role models for handling anger well, but some biblical characters do, while others make me feel less alone in my condition! Elisha seems to lose his temper. His mentor Elijah has just been taken up and he is still grieving the loss (2 Kings 2:1 – 13). His first journey is to the area of Bethel which is the site at which King Jeroboam had set up golden calves and established a place of Baal worship. Elisha comes to confront the power of Baal in the spirit of his teacher, Elijah. As he goes toward Bethel a group of young men seek to hinder his mission. They urge him to go away and bypass their pagan worship site. They resort to name calling in order to demean the prophet and disparage his message. He is met with derisive catcalls "Go away, Baldy!" Elisha soon has enough of their taunts and hindrance. Perhaps remembering how decisively his teacher had dealt with a group of prophets of Baal, Elisha calls down God's wrath on this group that have sought to hinder him and have personally insulted him.

Two bears emerge from the nearby woods and mauled forty-two of the young men. I note that nowhere in the narrative does it say that they were devoured but asserts they were mauled. When I first learned this story in Sunday School, the main teaching point was that we ought to respect our elders. I admit I was envious of Elisha since there were several people in my life who I might like to see mauled. I came to quite like this mercurial prophet and his temperament. Over the years as my forehead continues to grow at the expense of my hairline, he and I have even more in common.

Paul's temper gets him in trouble as well(Acts 16). He and Silas are in Phillipi sharing the Word of the Lord and they are constantly interrupted by a young slave girl, who has a "spirit of divination." She keeps calling out "These men are servants of the Most High God." Paul finally becomes exasperated and tells her to be quiet and orders the evil spirit out of her. The owners of the slave girl having lost their chief source of revenue cause Paul and Silas to be arrested, flogged, and imprisoned. Paul's pique of temper has consequences, but God has plans. A whole jail, the jailer and his family are saved as time plays out. God brings good out of even this dangerous emotion.

Good has not always come from my forays into anger, other than expensive lessons learned, but I have hope that there are godly uses for a right kind of anger. Before I act I find it best, now, to seek God and consider the consequences whether they be bad or good!

DAY 13

A Look From God's Point of View
Judges 6 & 7

THERE IS A TERM "ANTIPHRASIS" WHICH MEANS TO USE AN expression where the exact opposite would be appropriate. Some examples are calling a large man "Tiny" or a bald man "Curly." The irony of this appeals to our sense of humour. Upon first reading I thought I saw such a term in the story of Gideon. The scene is set in Israel, and the Midianites are in the habit of sweeping down from the hill country at harvest time each year and carrying off the produce and the women of Israel. Gideon has harvested some wheat and has set about 'threshing' it. This involves flailing it in order to separate the heavier wheat kernel from the lighter chaff. The kernels would then be milled into flour for baking. This regular farm activity was taking place in an unusual locale. Rather than a 'threshing floor' Gideon is threshing in a winepress! Not only was this an unusual place to thresh wheat it was a terribly inconvenient spot for this activity which demands a more spacious venue. We are told that Gideon is in these cramped quarters "to keep it from the Midianites."

It is upon this scene that the Lord appears and announces Himself. "The Lord is with you, mighty warrior." "Mighty warrior"? Is God using an antiphrase? It sure seems like it at first glance. Gideon is hardly the picture of a warrior let alone a mighty one, as he cowers in his winepress protecting his meagre gleanings. While his precautions are human and understandable they do not merit the accolades expressed from the Lord. Does God have his divine tongue in his celestial cheek?

The answer upon careful reading, is not. God sees beyond Gideon's obvious frailties. He identifies him by the as yet untapped potential which God himself placed there.

I give myself a pass for laughing at the seemingly ludicrous description of Gideon, for Gideon himself was slow to believe. This cowerer became a conqueror. God patiently walked Gideon through doubt and fear and Gideon, in the strength of the Lord, delivered Israel from the oppression of the enemy.

There remains much humour in the story of Gideon's transformation, but that is for another day. My big take away from this encounter is that when God's calls us "Beloved" or "more than conquerors" He does so from the knowledge that He has made us to fit that description. By His hand he can transform us "from glory to glory." Early in the Bible (Genesis 16:13) Hagar glorifies God proclaiming "You are the God who sees me." God sees me and still loves me and calls me "beloved." Let us not scoff or laugh at God's description of us, but rather lean into it, and live out the depiction. Lives of faith are lives believing that what God says is true!

If you quiet your heart and mind you can hear the still small voice calling you "mighty warrior."

DAY 14

The Mighty Warrior In Action
Judges 6:25 - 32

AFTER SOME SERIOUS CONVINCING, THE 'MIGHTY WARRIOR' TAKES his first steps toward fulfilling his potential. The area had become littered with Asherah poles. These were pagan totems which represented Israel's departure from the sole worship of the God of Abraham, Isaac, and Jacob. Gideon's first task was to tear one down.

It causes me amusement to picture this 'hero' of the faith sneaking out under cover of darkness as his inaugural step as 'mighty warrior.' He has emerged from cowering in a winepress, but his sneaking obedience is less than inspiring!

With the dawn of the new day the Baal worshippers arrive upon the scene of destruction of their Asherah pole. Word soon leaks that it was Gideon who did it. All his stealth did not avail. Soon a mob shows up at Gideon's home ready to stone him. Our 'mighty warrior' is found cowering again, as he hides behind his daddy who answers the door. Dad sends the mob packing telling them if Baal is really a god then leave vengeance to him "Let Baal contend!" As they slink off our not so intrepid hero is given a new nickname Jerub-Baal which means "let Baal contend."

I smile at Gideon knowing that better is in store for him. He has taken comic baby steps of obedience and ultimately he will take great strides in becoming all that God has called him to be. Though God used his father to rescue him Gideon is gaining a reputation and an unmerited nickname. God is preparing him for great things.

I sometimes watch You Tube videos of babies laughing if I need a smile. I also love to see babies' comic first steps as they totter and face plant. First steps are rarely sterling successes, but they form a 'watershed moment.' Life changes with that first step!

I laugh abashedly as I recall my first ham-fisted attempts to share God's story. I cringe and chuckle to remember my first sermon. I was awful! Yet those halting laughable acts of obedience were clearly 'watershed' moments. We may risk our dignity by stepping out in obedience, but we are opening the door to blessing and usefulness. Babies bravely take that step, maybe I should too.

DAY 15

The Mighty Warrior's Weapons
Judges 6: 33 – 7:22

PAUL WRITES IN 2 CORINTHIANS 10:4, "THE WEAPONS OF OUR warfare are not carnal (fleshly)" and we see that played out in scripture. David faces the giant with a slingshot and five smooth stones. Moses has a walking stick in the courts of mighty Pharoh. Perhaps the most comic weapons wielded were those of Gideon.

Our hero has put God to the test, inviting Him to alternately wet and keep dry a fleece. This is not a recommended practice for in this case God reciprocates and tests Gideon. Jesus during the temptations makes it abundantly clear that we are not to "test the Lord your God."

Gideon has established a reputation among the people of Israel, for when he calls for men to join his army over thirty-two thousand responded! At this point comes Gideon's first test.

God informs him he has too many men. If he were to free the people from the oppressors with that number the people might not recognize that it was, in fact, God who was their Rescuer. He tells Gideon to let anyone who is afraid to go home with his blessing. Can you imagine Dwight D. Eisenhower sharing a like message to the men of the Allied Forces before storming the beaches of Normandy? The idea is ludicrous and comic, to all our human (carnal) thinking.

Gideon's faith is tested, but he sends home twenty-two thousand soldiers. With over two thirds of his army gone Gideon sets forth but again God halts them. He tells Gideon there are still too many. Gideon's next test is to separate out those who will go with him against the Midianites and those he will discharge home. The Israelite forces march in the heat until they come to a stream. Seven hundred of the thousand men plunge their faces in the cool water and lap up the water thirstily. The other three hundred knelt and with cupped hands brought the water to their lips. God said "with the three hundred men... I will save you."

Gideon sent the seven hundred home and proceeded with the remainder. The original army of over thirty thousand was reduced by over ninety nine percent! Gideon and his little army finally come to the Midianite encampment. They are vastly outnumbered, but God is not through with his strange battle plan. The three hundred are to stealthily surround the Midianite camp. Gideon, at God's direction furnished each soldier with a horn and a torch encased in empty jars. The soldiers' hands were full with these and no sword or spear was drawn. At the signal from Gideon, they were to blow their horns, break their jars exposing the flaming torches, and to shout "For the Lord and for Gideon!"

When facing a mighty foe this seemed like an inadequate strategy, but it sent the Midianites into paroxysm of panic. The Midianites fled in fright and Gideon and his band of men returned victorious. He proved to be the "mighty warrior" not through weapons of warfare but rather through weapons of faith. At the end of this saga, we see that what God saw in Gideon was real and through faith in action the cowering Gideon was transformed into the mighty warrior.

Too often God's people are paralysed and exhibit inaction but, God continues to call, and he continues to equip. It is ours to exercise faith, and to put faith in action.

DAY 16

Picture This!
Matthew 21:1 - 11

I COME FROM A STORY TELLING FAMILY. MY PARENTS WERE FORMED by "The Golden Age" of radio where the listener's imagination was an important means of carrying the story. My father especially loved to tell stories that captured my young imagination. Peals of laughter often rang from our dinner table as we each imagined the picture his story would paint. One of my favourite television characters is Sophia from the show 'Golden Girls.' She would tell stories that began with the phrase "Picture this!" This catchphrase was an invitation to imagination.

I can never picture the instructions of a 'How To Manual' but I always arise to a challenge to imagine.

In recent years I was pleasantly surprised to learn that Saint Ignatius had developed a potent form of spirituality in which imagination was central. He invites us to read Scripture with imagination. I had been having fun with this exercise privately for years but now it was given legitimacy!

Often this way of engaging the Bible leads me to amusing pictures that tickle me. Such a story is that of Jesus' Triumphal Entry into Jerusalem, on Palm Sunday.

I picture it like this. Jerusalem was teeming with people from all over as Jesus approached riding on the foal of a donkey. As he was still a ways down the dusty road Bartimaeus, the relentless former blind beggar, spotted him and informed the previously mute man from Tyre, who begins to shout Jesus' praises. Zacchaeus was in his favoured spot, up a tree, and began to cut palm branches and hand them down to the man who earlier had a withered arm.

Legion who had roamed the tombs of Decapolis in nakedness, is the first to remove his cloak. Elderly shepherds who had witnessed the Heavenly Hosts outside Bethlehem break into songs of their own. Healed lepers, free from lives of isolation joined the throng. The lame jig with glee. Lazarus and the widow's son from Nain greet the Lord of Life. Children whom He had blessed joined the joyful reception!

A picture of the 'Church of Christ' appears as a token of what will be. The broken and the sin-stained rise with joy to meet the one who heals and forgives.

The only sour note in this symphony was from the rigid religious. To them the raucous welcome was unseemly. They urge Jesus to hush the crowd. Instead, Jesus quiets them by telling them that if this 'happy band of the healed' were quiet, that the rocks would cry out!

Much of the above springs from my imagination. The details are not dependable, but the Saviour is entirely trustworthy. My imaginings help me to know Him better and love him more deeply. I smile, inwardly, as I picture the delicious irony of my cast of characters, and I wonder where I would fit best in this pageant.

DAY 17

Sons of Thunder
Mark 3:17

I was new to the Cree community of Wemindji and early one morning I decided to go for a jog. I should have known better for Proverbs 28:1 tells us "The wicked run when no one is chasing them." As I ran the dusty road a single dog took interest and then he was joined by another. Soon a pack of excited canines were following close behind me. Northern dogs are not as domesticated as their southern kin. In my imagination they were reminiscent of wolves more than pooches. Soon my jog morphed into a sprint. It became abundantly clear that I was not going to outrun this pack. In desperation I came to a halt and turned to face this snarling crowd. I am not sure why, but I snarled and growled back at them. They too stopped and looked perplexed. I was ruining the fun of the chase. One by one they seemed to shrug off and I was left to walk home.

Little did I know, I was watched through windows and those watching were highly amused. I was given a nickname to commemorate the occasion. As I entered the Bay Store or walked down the street I would often hear people use this same Cree expression often accompanied by a chuckle. Not until my last day in the community did I learn what my Cree moniker was. I was called "The man who barks at dogs." The name was given out of teasing but became a kind of term of affection. I had earned it!

John the Gospel writer has been given a number of nicknames, "the disciple Jesus loved," and the Apostle of Love are two memorable ones. My favourite though was given him by Jesus himself. He called John and his brother James "Sons of Thunder." At the time of designating these two with this name there is no apparent reason but in the same way that He knew Nathaniel was "a man in whom there is no guile" he knew these fellows' temperament. They display this thunderous nature when filled with anger they seek the power to call down fire from heaven upon some inhospitable Samaritans.

I take great solace in learning that 'the Apostle of Love' was once a 'Son of Thunder.' It demonstrates God's power to transform even an angry nature. As a person who has a natural bent to the volatile, I find hope in the dramatic change that results from following Jesus and walking in his way.

While in that same Cree community I once had occasion to call a church member. Her daughter answered the phone. I had been instructing this girl in 'Moral and Religious Education' in the local school. She exclaimed to her mother, "It's that Red Flaming." Perhaps I had earned yet another nickname, like John, based on my temperament! Years later I hope there is less of 'Red Flaming' and more of Jesus.

DAY 18

Heroes Anonymous
John 11:1 - 44

HEBREWS CHAPTER ELEVEN IS OFTEN CALLED THE "FAITH HALL OF Fame." In this chapter the writer list a number of Bible heroes and a recitation of their deeds. While I find these giants of the faith inspiring, I want to advocate for an equally inspiring contingent. I think we should create an "Heroes Anonymous Hall of Fame." This 'hall' would be filled with the nameless, faceless individuals who contribute to the story of Scripture.

Abraham, Noah, Moses, and David all have epic stories of faith but the average Christian does not lead an 'epic' life! An ordinary hero is perhaps more to our tastes. Someone who performs in a manner we can identify with, or a role-model we can aspire to, may suit us better.

My first nominees for the "Heroes Anonymous Hall of Fame" appear in John chapter eleven. The named characters are Jesus, Mary, Martha, and the recently deceased Lazarus. Jesus arrives on the scene of sorrow. He is too late to prevent Lazarus' death. He has been entombed for four days and his sisters and their friends are in deep mourning. Jesus only seems late. His timing is perfect no matter our expectations. He comforts the sisters and then directs that the stone sealing Lazarus' tomb be rolled away.

This is when our anonymous heroes enter the picture. These unnamed folk have some vital functions to play! They put their backs to the task given. It does not take either skill or extraordinary faith. They simply obey and do what is in their power to do. They roll away the stone. Later in the Gospel the task of stone rolling is supernatural but here is ordinary human effort on display. Without this human obedience the next part would be entirely different for Jesus calls the corpse to life and commands Lazarus to come out.

The crowd was startled as Lazarus, still entangled by the grave clothes, emerges out of the tomb. I picture Lazarus swaddled in burial wrappings which had encased spices, hopping (imagine a potato sack race) out! Now our anonymous heroes go into action once more. While Eminem and the Notorious B.I.G may be great rappers these unidentified folks become the great unwrappers!

At Jesus' command they loose the enlivened Lazarus, freeing him from the final marks of death that remained. Like the stone rolling this is both a simple and important task.

Jesus does all the hard stuff. He alone can bring life to the dead. We might recall that he earlier asserted "I am the resurrection and the life." The anonymous, nameless, and faceless heroes contribute what they can and together they see the miraculous happen.

Paul tells us that before Christ made us alive, we were dead in our sin and trespasses. Christ alone, through faith alone, brings us to life! We emerge with Him from the tomb but remain encumbered by what the writer of Hebrews describes as "the sin that so easily entangles." It remains the task of anonymous heroes, you and me, to assist in removing these 'grave clothes' and we require each other because we too need help with ours.

There are those who believe they can live a Christian life apart from the Church without realizing the indispensable place that the anonymous heroes of the Church fill.

These folks are a potent example to me. I will likely never part a sea or build an ark in the desert but there are things I can do, and what I can do, I ought to do, so that Jesus' divine power can be loosed in the lives of those around. These are role-models indeed! (and in deed).

DAY 19

The Heart of the Matter
1 Samuel 15:16 - 23

I HAVE ALWAYS LOVED READING. YOU CAN LEARN A LOT FROM books! Early in my reading career I would pick books by their look or titles. We had a little mobile library that would park across the street from my home. At age ten I picked up a biography of Martin Luther, one of the leading lights of the Reformation. The book was way above my head but I picked it because as I looked at the Table of Contents, I spied that one chapter was entitled "The Diet of Worms." I was caught up with boyish anticipation of Luther's gross eating habits and I was terribly deflated to learn that a Diet was a meeting and Worms was a town in which the convention took place!

Portia in Shakespeare's 'Merchant of Venice' says, "All that glisters is not gold." Author George Eliot penned the phrase "Never judge a book by its cover." We can be easily taken in by appearances. Our culture may call things beautiful that have nothing lasting or virtuous about them. We are slow to learn Portia's lesson or to apply Eliot's truism. We fall for the 'glister' and embrace the beauty of the 'cover' only to be disappointed like a ten-year-old boy who finds Luther did not digest squigglies.

Even a great spiritual figure like the Prophet Samuel was prey to this temptation. He had earlier discerned God's choice for the first King of Israel. He had anointed King Saul. Saul was a singular individual! He stood head and shoulders above his countrymen. He had regal bearing that seemed to confirm his calling. However, Saul eventually became disobedient and ultimately deranged.

It became Samuel's task to anoint Saul's replacement. God led him to the family of Jesse in Bethlehem. Immediately he spots Jesse's oldest son and he too has the regal bearing. It is obvious to Samuel that he has witnessed the new king. Here Samuel exhibits wisdom we would do well to heed. He consults with God perhaps thinking God will endorse his choice. God though surprises Samuel, "Do not consider his appearance or his height, for I have rejected him." God goes on to say, "People look at outward appearance, but the LORD looks at the heart." Jesse parades son after son before the prophet. After the seventh walked before Samuel and God had not affirmed any of them, Samuel in exasperation asks if there are any more sons of Jesse. Jesse admits there is one more. He is the youngest and the runt of the litter. He is out taking care of the sheep. Jesse is sure that young David is not kingly material. Samuel requests that the lad be brought to him. Jesse sent for David, and as soon as the young boy came into sight God spoke to Samuel. "Rise and anoint him; this is the one!"

It appears God wanted a Shepherd King and saw in David a man after his own heart. David has a checkered record as King. He often failed, but always returned in faith and trust. This flawed Shepherd King becomes a foreshadow of the Good Shepherd and King of Kings and Lord of Lords. The ancestor is eclipsed by descendant.

In the world of the church, we are often attracted by the glitter and caught up in the new and exciting looking thing. We are called by God to take up our cross and follow Jesus. The cross is a hideous symbol of death with no worldly attraction in it. I cannot pursue the glittering things of the world and the cross at the same time. One seems more alluring but Portia, Eliot and God remind me that appearance can be deceiving. A friend of mine, George Eves, often reminded us "The heart of the matter is the matter of the heart!" It is here God looks! Have I set my heart after the things of God?

DAY 20

Lesson in Witness
John 9:1 - 34

I HEARTILY ENJOYED THE BILL MURRAY MOVIE "WHAT ABOUT BOB?" In this film Murray plays Bob Wiley, a patient being treated by Dr. Leo Marvin played by Richard Dreyfuss. Eventually Bob is recognized as the sane one and Leo is reduced to a catatonic state.

I take great heart that God has declared that He will use the foolish to confound the wise. This promise gives me hope that I can have a positive impact for the Kingdom despite my flaws and foolishness.

John chapter nine comically demonstrates this principle in action. Jesus comes across a man who had been born blind. The Lord of Compassion takes pity on this man and is moved to an unique form of action. He spits! With the spit and the ubiquitous dust, he makes a paste and smears it on the man's unseeing eyes! He commands, "Go, wash in the pool of Siloam." Anxious to rid his eyes of this unpleasant goop the man does as Jesus said and returns seeing for the very first time!

People stare at him wondering if this is the fellow who had been born blind. He was happy to tell them that it was indeed he. They asked how this had happened opening his first opportunity to witness to Jesus' miracle working power. He does not exaggerate but simply recites the facts of his healing.

His second opportunity comes when the people of the crowd take him to the Pharisees, for their expert opinion of these events. Again, he humbly retells the events involved. The experts are full of questions. Surely they reason this cannot be from God because this healing work was done on the Sabbath! As their disputation progressed, they turned again to the man born blind. His response boiled down to "All I know is, I was blind and now I see."

The experts next gambit was to suggest that this was not the same man who was born blind. They send for his parents. It appears that the blind man may have inherited his plain manner of speaking. "This is our son." they said. "We do not know how he was healed." "Ask him."

Perplexed the experts call the man before them again and for a third time he witnessed to the miracle and the Miracle Worker! He even asked if they wanted to become His disciples. The experts vehemently declined that opportunity but later the man had an opportunity of his own. He finally met Jesus and saw Him for the first time, his response was "Lord, I believe." And he worshiped Him.

The experts are left in the futility of their thinking while the simple man finds truth and life.

My father had a tongue in cheek expression, "You could almost write a book about things I don't know." In saying this he acknowledged that there were many things he did not know. I share that not so rare quality. I am no expert!

This lack of expertise can sometimes cause us to feel inadequate and silence our witness. 'The Man Born Blind' shows us the way. I can say like Hank Williams "I saw the Light!" Jesus has touched me and brought me to life. People can argue about theology, but my experience of the Lord is mine and is inarguable. This I can share confidently and simply.

DAY 21

Philip the Role Model
Acts 8:26 - 40

INCONGRUITY IS THE BASIS FOR MUCH HUMOUR, FROM THE TIME that Mom first disappears behind the baby blanket and reappears seconds later with a smiling "Peekaboo!," we find the unexplained and out of context funny.

Philip is the archetypical Evangelist. In fact, he is the only Bible character given that title. We first meet him as he is appointed one of the seven deacons in Acts chapter 6. He is a Greek speaking Jew who is identified as wise and compassionate. He and his cohorts are charged with addressing injustices on behalf of the Greek speaking widows. Later we see him during a persecution of the Church. He and others scatter taking with them the gospel message. Under Philip's care a great revival breaks out in Samaria. People are coming to faith and God is healing and restoring. When Philip's success in ministry became known, the Apostles in Jerusalem sent Peter and John to investigate.

Instead of basking in the glow of this success Philip, sensitive to the Holy Spirit, answered a call to go out to the desert road. Could a more drastic change be imagined? Philip left an exciting movement of the Holy Spirit of God and travelled to the dry, desolate, and lifeless desert road. Here he sees a cloud of dust arising as a chariot begins to roll by. Ever attentive Philip hears "Go to that chariot and stay near it." Philip obeys and it is now that the 'amusement' begins!

Philip runs! This is not a dignifying activity for a revival leader but he runs. Now if we are not careful we will not note that the driver of the chariot does not stop right away. Philip runs alongside and hears the Ethiopian reading Scripture. "Do you understand?" Philip asks in a panting voice as he continues to jog alongside. Eventually the chariot is paused for Philip to join the Ethiopian. He begins right where the man was reading and shared the good news with him. Like the Samaritans earlier in the story this gentleman comes to the point of faith. Philip has again demonstrated his bona fides as "Philip the Evangelist." They come upon some water and the Ethiopian asks to be baptised, as a mark of this newfound faith, and Philip obliges.

As in his time in Samaria, Philips task is done and he is whisked off on his next adventure.

The picture of Philip running strikes me as funny. In the heat of the Middle East on a desert road, with his skirts tucked up Philip literally comes alongside and remains alongside until he has a Spirit led opportunity to share the faith. Dust covered and sweat caked he runs! Undignified, he runs! In obedience and faith, he runs. Gasping he listens and puffing he shares!

I can not imagine a more apt model for evangelism. He is compassionate, he cares for the lost. He is sensitive to the Spirit's prompting, and instant in obedience, ready to go to the inhospitable places. He goes to great and uncomfortable lengths to come alongside and 'hear.' He follows the advice of 1 Peter 3:15 and is always prepared to share the hope he himself has and to do so with gentleness and respect. He did not bask in success but entrusted those he had led to others so that he could pursue the next adventure God had for him, no matter where that might be.

Over my forty years plus as an Evangelist, I have not found a better role-mode than this comic character, huffing and puffing beside a lone chariot on a dry and dusty road. I have found myself in many uncomfortable and laughable (in hind sight) situations as I have attempted to walk in the giant foot steps of Philip the Evangelist.

DAY 22

Elijah the Trash Talker
1 Kings 18: 20 - 40

FROM THE TIME I FIRST SAID, "I'M THE KING OF THE CASTLE AND you're the dirty rascal!" I have had an appreciation for what is called 'trash talk.' Trash talk is teasing or taunting rhetoric designed to elevate one's achievement. Some trash talk is repugnant but really good trash talk is clever and contains humour.

Elijah in his encounter with King Ahab and the Prophets of Baal is a sterling example of 'holy trash talk.' Ahab begins by calling Elijah "a trouble maker." Elijah comes back "I have not made trouble for Israel but you and your father's family have." Then Elijah 'throws down his challenge.' He defies Ahab to assemble all of Baal's prophets for a winner take all contest. The king cannot let this challenge go unanswered so he calls a convocation of all the prophets of Baal from throughout the Kingdom.

Great crowds turn out to witness the contest. Elijah addresses the throng, "How long will you waver between two opinions?" He then suggests they settle the matter to see if the Lord God of Israel or Baal is the one true God.

The two opponents each set up an altar and prepare a sacrifice. They pile the wood ready for ignition but do not set it afire. Elijah's contest is to see whose God will be able to light the flame and burn the sacrifice. Ahab's team of prophets get first crack at the task. For the next six hours these 'prophets' jump and dance and plead with their god to show up in power, but there is no response! The time has arrived for Elijah to begin his epic 'trash talk.'

"Shout louder. Maybe your god is sleeping!" The 'prophets' redoubled their efforts yelling louder and cutting themselves with swords and spears in order to move their so far unmoving god. As it was starting to get dark Elijah began to take his turn. He heaped injury on his insults by having four huge buckets of water poured over his wood and sacrifice. He had the crowd's attention now! Then he had another four buckets poured over just to drive home the point and did it yet a third time! Then the Prophet of God prayed "Answer me, Lord, answer me, so these people will know that you LORD, are God." Then, like a Jerry Lee Lewis song, came great balls of fire that consumed the wood, the sacrifice and lapped up the water.

The late great baseball pitcher Dizzy Dean said, "It ain't bragging if you can do it." Elijah knew that the LORD was God. This was ultimately no contest. When Jesus invites us to call on His name, He is inviting us to prove once again that He is Lord and that any other powers in this world are impotent in comparison with Him.

Elijah listened to the promptings of the Holy Spirit and then boldly stepped out in prayer. The 'trash talk' was but an evidence of Elijah's utter confidence, not in his own powers, but in the all-powerful Lord.

DAY 23

Balaam's Ass
Numbers 22: 21 - 38

THE STORY OF BALAAM AND HIS ASS IS FULL OF IRONIC HUMOUR and it became the basis of a memorably funny incident in my own life.

Balaam has been gifted by God with the ability to 'tell forth the Word of the Lord.' In some ways he is an object lesson that being given a gift does not equate to personal holiness. We can easily confuse these two and it sometimes does great harm to the Church and to individuals when we exalt people without proven character, purely on the basis of charisma. Balaam is a very flawed prophet. He seems to be more interested in profit and sets out to be a prophet for hire. As it turns out Balak the King of the Midianites, Israel's longtime enemy, is in the market for a freelance prophet. Balaam is offered a princely sum to put a curse on the army of Israel. Perhaps, as a negotiating strategy Balaam demurred, but finally agrees to accompany Balak, and see what he can do.

He sets off with the intent of satisfying Balak and getting paid. The Lord, who knows our hearts, was angered at this attitude of willful disobedience. The angel of the Lord waited on the road to ambush the profligate prophet. Balaam, who was a 'seer' of sorts did not apprehend the angel and was blithely headed for his doom.

His donkey though saw what Balaam could not and refused to go forward! Balaam lost it on the donkey, severely beating it with his staff.

Then something happened that the 'seer' never saw coming. God enabled the donkey to speak. "What have I done to make you beat me?" Balaam by this point is so angry he does not even pause at the wonder of his donkey talking, but instead replies to it "You have made a fool of me!" Then the Lord opened Balaam's eyes and he saw the angel standing in front of him with a sword in hand, and he manages to avoid certain death.

The story ends with the greedy prophet unable to curse the Israelite army but he shares a strategy by which Midian might seduce Israel into sin.

As a young boy I watched Mr. Ed the talking horse and Saturday television matinees of Francis the Talking Mule. When I discovered this story of Balaam I recognized its humour immediately.

Much to my teachers' dismay and fellow students' delight I have long practised injecting humour in solemn and serious moments and the story of Balaam's Ass gave me a golden opportunity.

I was working as an Evangelist. My friend Bruce Smith and I were leading an evangelistic event in a church in Windsor Ontario. I preached the first night and while the hymn before the message was being played, Bruce came over and quietly prayed for me. This thoughtful gesture is typical of Bruce who is a gentle and holy man.

The next night it was Bruce's turn to preach and it was my turn to quietly pray for him but I could not resist some good-natured fun. I whispered in Bruce's ear, "Remember Balaam's Ass, if God could speak through it He will surely speak through you!" Stifling a laugh Bruce ascended the pulpit to proclaim the Word.

I used to tell a riddle "How is the Church like the mighty Mackenzie River?" The answer is "They are both often frozen at the mouth!" The story of Balaam's donkey ought to encourage us to open our mouths and share with an unseeing world the truth of God's love.

DAY 24

The Spit Take
Revelation 3:14 - 22

ONE OF THE OLDEST 'SIGHT GAGS' PROBABLY ORIGINATED AROUND caveman cook fires. Modern comedians have used it as a laugh getting shtick. It is the 'spit take'! A spit take is a comic technique of suddenly spitting out liquid one is drinking in response to something funny or surprising. It was a standard in Vaudeville and has often found its way into television situation comedies.

I used to enjoy making my siblings laugh at dinner time. I would time my 'bit' for when someone's mouth was full (milk was the best)with hopes of making them spew it or better yet to 'snort' liquid through the nose. I got great amusement from this but it did not always strike my parents as that delightful.

Like most 'slap stick' comedy there is a repulsive but "can not look away" quality to spit takes. It is juvenile but touches something basic in us that causes enjoyment.

Scripture has Jesus doing a holy spit take. In this case though there is no humour!

The Lord is addressing the Church of the city Laodicea, in Revelation chapter three "I know your deeds, that you are neither cold nor hot. I wish you were one or the other! So, because you are lukewarm – neither cold nor hot – I am about to spit you out of my mouth."

Here Jesus addresses a complacent church, a church that enjoys all the material blessings and has taken these for granted. Gratitude and love have grown cold! They have allowed themselves to become lulled into a stupor. They are in that most dangerous of positions, they are lost and do not know it. There is hope for the 'prodigal' to come to himself and return but the lukewarm apathy of the Laodiceans is perilous!

Here we have revulsion without redeeming humour. There is nothing remotely funny about their situation. It is deadly serious! Jesus pronounces that like lukewarm water this church will be spewed out.

In His compassion though, Jesus does not leave them without hope. He shares one more picture with them. He is standing outside this 'church.' What a terrible state for a church to be in, that Jesus is relegated to the outside. The Old Testament has a word "Ichabod" which means "the glory has departed." Here in Revelation chapter three, we see this vivid picture. The Lord is on the outside of His church saying, "Here I am! I stand at the door and knock." There is a famous painting by Holman Hunt "The Light of the World" which depicts this scene. In the painting there is no knob on the outside of the door. If Jesus is to have entrée to the church once more it must be at their express invitation. Unlike the SWAT teams of movies and television, Jesus will not barge in uninvited. Like the consummate gentleman He knocks. In knocking He invites the lukewarm church back to intimate fellowship with Him once more.

There is no situation beyond the Redeemer's reach. The invitation to hear this knock is universal but each individual must make the choice. The offer of loving relationship is made and must be personally appropriated.

I learned around my childhood dining table, that decisions have consequences. Making my sister snort milk through her nose might well lead to banishment from the table. It seemed a worthwhile bargain at the time. Living apart from Jesus now has consequences too, if we choose to live apart from Him, He will honour our choice and we will spend our eternity apart from the one Holman Hunt rightly titled "The Light of the World." This is a spit take we want no part for ourselves, nor do we want this future for those we love. We then ought to show and tell of the Saviour's love and invitation so others find that same intimate fellowship which enlivens us.

DAY 25

A Case of Mistaken Identity
John 20:11 - 18

ONE OF SHAKESPEARE'S GREAT COMEDIES IS "COMEDY OF ERRORS." The whole story is carried by the idea of mistaken identity. We are introduced to two sets of twins: Antipholus of Syracuse and Antipholus of Ephesus and their servants Dromio of Syracuse and Dromio of Ephesus. The mistake takes five acts to untangle during which much hilarity ensues.

Several years ago, someone offered our ministry a plot of ground to be used as a community garden, This property was strewn with garbage and filled with huge rocks. It was also the litterbox of a community of feral cats. An educated horticulturalist might well have passed on the offer, but I unschooled in the science of agriculture saw possibilities.

Over the next few years, through dint of effort and an out pouring of sweat capital (literally) we turned that vacant lot into a sad and sorry excuse for a garden. We were happy to hear the land had been sold to a developer and the gardening could not continue.

During this period of time, I used to say that I felt particularly close to Christ. We had both been mistaken for gardeners!

In Jesus' case the mistake occurred not in a toxic urban plot but outside his very own tomb. He had been crucified on what we call Good Friday and now on the first day of the week Mary of Magdala has come to mourn and minister to the Saviour's body. She has found the tomb empty and assumed (you know what they say about assuming) that someone has made off with the corpse. With tear filled eyes she spies the 'gardener' and implores him to tell her where they have taken Jesus' body.

He too was mistaken for a gardener!

When Jesus called her by name, "Mary", suddenly her heart succeeded where her eyes failed. This was the Lord, miraculously alive!

While his death offers atonement to 'whosoever' it is received personally. No one has a birthright to redemption. Like Mary each of us responds individually. Each is offered a personal encounter with the Risen Lord, with all the benefits of his passion, but we must personally respond. Just as being born in hospital does not make you a nurse so being born in a Christian family does not make you a Christian. This gift is universally offered and individually obtained.

Have you, Dear Reader, like Mary, had a personal encounter with the Risen Lord? If not, today can be your day! He is only a prayer away, waiting for you to call on his Name to find forgiveness, life, and peace. Any pretense that I was a gardener was easily dismissed but Jesus promises a fruitful life, lived in his power. Now that is a Master Gardner!

DAY 26

Good News
Mark 1:14 - 15

I GOT MY FIRST JOB EARLY IN LIFE. AT AGE TWELVE I BECAME A paper boy. Perhaps this foreshadowed my lifelong involvement in sharing 'Good News.' I liked the quiet of the early mornings and the solitude of those peaceful dawns. I shared a small bedroom with three brothers and always enjoyed 'alone time' when I could get it. The one aspect I did not like was winter. The onset of winter meant that it was time to put away my bike and trudge the route in heavy snow boots. I resisted this reality as long as I could.

One blustery November day I awoke to an icy, frozen world, and knew I should deliver the papers on foot, but I decided to try riding my bicycle on the wintry roads. I placed the heavy bundle in the carrier on the handle bars and set off. I managed to slip and slide safely for the first while but soon wiped-out going around a corner. The gusting wind took my papers and strewed them the length and breadth of the chain link fence around the local high school. They were soggy and scattered beyond saving! I picked up myself and my bike and plodded home. I explained to my mom what had happened. She drove me to the sight of the debacle and soon agreed with me that these papers were irretrievable. She drove me into town to an all-night convenience store where we purchased replacement newspapers and I finished my deliveries on foot.

When I got home our phone started to ring. Unhappy customers wanted to know why they had received yesterday's paper! I let my mom explain, but not only was I out the cost of the papers that had blown away but also the replacement papers I could not charge them for.

My weekly profits were gone. It was a costly mistake to try and ride that day.

The 'news' I had delivered that morning was anything but new! Mark says of Jesus' initial ministry that he "… went into Galilee, proclaiming the good news of God." The Good News is that in the person of Jesus the Kingdom of God has come near and that through Him we can have access to the life this fallen world can never offer. The Good News that God has provided the answer, Jesus, to the human dilemma.

I am so grateful for a Sunday School teacher, Miss Crump, who shared this Good News with me. She was an elderly woman (perhaps my current age) and was confined to a wheelchair. I do not know how she did it but week after week she met with a group of us in the church basement and shared the love of God with us. I received that life changing Good News and have never regretted it.

Soon our little church recognized something in me and at a Confirmation Service prayed for God's calling on my life.

Over the many years since I have tried to remain a deliverer of the Good News, that so changed my life! There have been mishaps and comic situations not dissimilar to my paper boy adventures, but it has been the 'ride of my life'! I highly recommend this Gospel calling, to share the Good News and invite you to join me in delivering this news to a world dying to hear. However, I do not recommend bicycling on icy roads.

DAY 27

Undone!
Isaiah 6:1 - 8

LIKE MOST OF MY CLOTHES AS A BOY, I WAS WEARING A 'NEW TO me' sweater. It was a warm woolen sweater that I imagine some grandmother somewhere had spent hours knitting. It was a frosty fall day when I decided to take a short cut across a field. I went over one strand of barbed wire and under another. I had walked some twenty feet beyond this barrier when I sensed something was wrong! I looked behind and saw a trail of red wool leading back to the fence. I looked down at my 'new' sweater and the waist was now at my rib cage. The sweater had snagged and unravelled. There was no way that I was ever going to fix this mess! There was nothing to do but face the music. Reluctantly I did that and received the "Money doesn't grow on trees." lecture, which I heard often growing up and I must admit gave to my own children in the years to come.

There is a terrible sinking feeling that comes with an unravelling but in Isaiah chapter six, Isaiah experiences a much worse 'unravelling.' He was in the temple when the atmosphere changed. He had a unique experience with the Holy God! The encounter involved an angelic seraphim choir, holy smoke, and trembling temple pillars!

Isaiah's response is "Woe is me! I am undone!" (Isaiah 6:5 KJV) This word "undone" has the sense of unravelling, like my sweater. It is an undoing beyond repair. His words describe the experience of a sinful soul in the presence of the Holy God.

This does not seem like 'good news' but a cure is not effective apart from diagnosis. Here Isaiah's experience is so intense and the diagnosis so apparent that in a moment of self-awareness he recognizes his utter sinfulness compared to the holiness of God. As the drama continues a coal from the fire is used to bring purity and allow Isaiah to continue in the Lord's presence. It is a picture of rightness being attributed at a cost. It seems a foreshadow of Jesus imputing righteousness to humans. He, in the flesh, accomplishes the atoning sacrifice by which we are able to stand in the presence of the Holy God, and not only stand but to boldly approach the throne room and address God as Abba (Daddy).

I had to face my mother with my undone-ness and I suffered my own consequences. The Good News is that as I face my undone-ness with God, Jesus bears the consequences. I can shed my righteousness, which is like filthy rags, and exchange them for pure robes of righteousness purchased for me by the sacrificial death of Christ, mine through His resurrection!

Now rather than being 'undone' I can stand "complete in Him." Now that is Good News!

DAY 28

In the Presence of Majesty
Hebrews 4:13

IN THE LATE 90'S I HAD AN UNEXPECTED ENCOUNTER WITH royalty. At the time one of my roles was as Prairie Regional Director of the Church Army in Canada. I got word that a team from Canada was to travel to England for a Church Army World Leaders Conference and I was to be included. When I received the itinerary one event stood out. We were to visit Queen Elizabeth II at Buckingham Palace!

My son, David, who was then in his early teens, had read in Uncle John's Bathroom Reader, that the Queen enjoyed crossword puzzles. As we were saying our good byes at the Winnipeg Airport, David disappeared into the little shop there and reappeared with a crossword magazine in hand. "Give this to the Queen for me, please." I tucked it into my carry-on bag and left.

As the time for the visit to the Palace came closer I was told by the chap in charge of arrangements that I ought not to give such a gift to the Queen, and that Church Army had gone to pains to have a special gift for Her Majesty.

On the morning of the visit, we made our way through a throng of tourists and were passed through the gates and ushered into the palace where we were to be greeted by the Queen. We were placed in a horse shoe around the hall. Finally, she entered and shook hands and chatted with each individual around the room. As she drew near, I was faced with a dilemma! Would I follow proper protocol and disappoint my son or would I risk the ire of the chap in charge.

When it was my turn to be introduced I whipped the magazine out of my pocket and offered it to the Queen on behalf of my son. We chatted a bit about him (I kept the Bathroom Reader bit to myself) and then she smiled and said, "I hope it is not too difficult." After I assured her that the answers were in the back we both smiled and she moved on. A few weeks later our little Prairie post office was abuzz! There were two letters postmarked Buckingham Palace. One was for me and one for David, thanking us for the crosswords! For a brief time, we were local celebrities.

While this was a memorable experience it will not be my last or best experience of majesty! We read earlier about Isaiah's encounter with the holiness and majesty of God. John in Revelation uses all sorts of brilliant imagery to portray the awesome majesty of God. Even more thrilling though is the writer of Hebrews who informs us that because of the finished work of Christ, we can "...approach God's throne of grace with confidence." Scripture is clear that one day we will all stand before the Judgement Seat of God. For those who have trusted in Jesus there need not be dismay but to those who trust in their own merit there is dread indeed!

The writer of Hebrews also informs us "Just as people are destined to die once, and after that to face judgement." The eternally vital question then is "Have you trusted Jesus?" It is not too late right now but it will be soon! You can settle that question before you move on to the next vignette. Please do.

DAY 29

Blissfully Unaware
Mark 4: 35 - 41

I WAS A RELATIVE NEWBIE TO FLYING. I HAD A COUPLE OF FLIGHTS on commercial airlines but this was my first experience in the co-pilot's seat. I was seated next to my friend Lars on his 1948 single engine Stinson float plane. We had taken off from the God's River and the community of Shamattawa, Manitoba, where I was spending the summer in youth ministry.

I was in awe for the whole flight. The view from this tiny plane was spectacular. Things became even more thrilling as we flew. We were soon encased in a dark rain cloud and bolts of lightning lit up the skies in front of our eyes. I had never seen the lightning and heard the "boom" simultaneously before. I was oohing and aahing throughout the trip. When we landed and Lars had cut the engine I began to put into words my delight at the display of wonder we had witnessed. As it turns out Lars was not nearly as thrilled as me. He informed me that while I was sublimely unaware that we were in mortal danger and that could he, he might have strangled me for my expressions of delight.

It seemed to annoy my friend that I did not share his sense of rising tension! My blissful ignorance of our situation only exaggerated his angst. In Mark chapter four, the seasoned sailors on Jesus' boat trip, must have felt the same. These experienced fishermen were caught in a violent storm which they recognized perilous. Meanwhile Jesus was enjoying a much-needed nap in the stern. They were aware enough of the seriousness of the situation to dread the inevitable outcome but to this dread was added the seeming indifference of their rabbi to their situation. They rouse Him to express their anger, not at the storm but at their Saviour.

We know the end of the story. Jesus calms the storm and they land ashore safe and sound, just as He had said they would at the onset of the trip. It is interesting to note though that their fear led them to blame Jesus. He not only rebukes the wind and waves but He rebukes them for their lack of trust. It is their own lack of faith that allowed panic to rise and even brought them to anger directed toward him.

I wonder how quick we are to blame God for the storms of life and rage against God rather than trust that God will bring us through whatever He may bring us to! Not all storms at sea have this happy ending. In Chapter six of Mark Jesus, instead of speaking to the circumstances, speaks to the disciples. He speaks His 'peace' into their frightened hearts. Not all planes land safely as we did through that electrical storm but those who are in Christ can rest in knowing that "underneath are the everlasting arms."

DAY 30

Falling and Folly
Luke 5: 1 - 8

I IMAGINE THE SCENE LIKE THIS: JESUS HAS INSTRUCTED HIS exhausted would-be disciples to put out once more in their boat. Though they have been fishing fruitlessly (Can one fish fruitlessly?) yet they obey. They return with an outlandish catch of fish! As they draw the nets to shore Simon Peter falls face first into the writhing mass of fish and begs of Jesus "Go away from me, Lord, I am a sinful man!"

With his face full of fragrant fish Peter demonstrates his position as a sinner in the presence of the Holy One. It tickles my funny bone to picture the scene like this. It is an apt picture of the "filthy rags" clad sinner in the presence of the pure and righteous Son of God! Peter falling on his face is not the sole fall in scripture. We have previously noted that falls can be a source of great humour if there is no real harm. In Acts chapter twenty we read about another fall.

Eutychus had probably worked all day and joined in an evening revival meeting where Paul was speaking. The meeting continued past dark and lamps were lit in the room. Eutychus retreated to a third story window sill for fresh air trying to stave off a set of heavy eyelids. Finally, he could not stay awake a moment longer and dropped off. He not only dropped off to sleep but he literally dropped off the window sill landing with a thud on the ground outside. A gasp filled the room and the meeting's attention was diverted to this dramatic accident. Paul went down and raised up the fallen man and restored him to the shaken community.

Because he was restored the situation has humour. Lessons may well have been learned by all. Paul may have learned to be briefer. The host may have been more careful of ventilation, and I am sure Eutychus never fell asleep during a sermon again.

Even painful falls which result in growth can be humorous. I had a serious life-threatening fall. My face was shattered, teeth knocked out, and I was well and truly concussed! I had taken a group from the inner-city on a holiday to Deer Island. I was determined to show them the joys of nature and one of my plans was to demonstrate flying a kite. This is an activity that none had participated in before. I went down to the 'beach' in hopes of catching a breeze. This is not normally a problem on the Fundy Shore. I managed to coax the kite up but my foot slipped on some of the rock weed on the water's edge. I could have and should have let go of the kite but I did not! With nothing to break my fall other than my face, I crashed into a jagged rock. This was to be a life altering moment.

Over the next months of recovery, I learned a number of valuable lessons. With my jaw wired shut I learned ventriloquism. In fact, the next Christmas I tried out my ventriloquism as a Gospel Presentation at a Taylor College Banquet Dinner. I also learned humility as for the first time in my memory I was weak and unable to manage for myself. I was physically idle for weeks on end and engaged in wonderful intimate conversation with my Heavenly Father.

After years of dentistry, I can smile at the scene of my kite flying. I am grateful for all I have experienced and learned. I am sure Eutychus' experience was similar.

DAY 31

Who Are You Fooling?
1 Corinthians 3:18

I WAS OFTEN ACCUSED OF BEING "THE CLASS CLOWN." I WAS OFTEN told to stop "fooling around." These descriptions and admonitions were not meant to be complimentary. As I grew up I did not so much stop being a jester but learned instead the value of being the 'clown.

In the times when kings were authoritarian figures with absolute power, there arose a counterpoint figure, the court jester. He through humour and sarcasm could speak truth to the powers that be when no one else dared. These clownish figures were the truth tellers of their age.

Wrong ideas can withstand rebellion and all sorts of opposition but they seldom survive being unmasked and skewered by humour. This was true then and it is today! When I was young I used to wield this power with a definite lack of wisdom. Teachers did not appreciate my signaling that they had become tedious and were 'losing the room,' or that they had left the door wide open for a play on words or a pun. I was very often punished for my unsophisticated clowning. I learned, ever so slowly that true foolishness needed to be exercised with wisdom. Foolishness is like manure. It needs to be used sparingly and spread carefully!

The Psalmist David writes in Psalm 14:1 "The fool says in his heart "There is no God."" This is a 'fool' without knowledge, who does not speak truth at all. Paul contrasts that with the "fool for Christ" who is a truth teller. The Fool for Christ is not an agent of the powerful but instead is a speaker of truth.

Solomon in the Book of Proverbs warns of the folly of the Godless fool thirty-six times. In 1 Corinthians 3:18 Paul contrasts the foolishness of being 'wise' in the ways of the present age with becoming fools (simple truth tellers) for Christ and thus demonstrating the wisdom of God and His plan of salvation.

To the World the Cross seems utter foolishness. It is an instrument of execution not exaltation. On Good Friday, the sky turned black. It seemed that Satan had won but God demonstrates the true foolishness of that thinking through the resurrection of Christ on Easter morning.

Few of us are powerful, influential, or wealthy, yet God delights in using the unexpected and ordinary Fool for Christ to share the truth. Remember Jesus said in John 14:6 "I am the Way, the Truth, and the Life..." No one no matter their rhetorical skill can refute our testimony that this Jesus has changed my life. For the most part, I am no longer the interrupting class clown but I do aspire to always be "A Fool for Christ." Some suggest that the Church is full of fools. I assert that is not true! There is always room for one more!

DAY 32

Beyond Your Wildest Dream
Romans 4:1 – 6 John 19: 20

SOMETIMES MEN STARE OFF INTO SPACE AND WHEN ASKED "WHAT are you thinking about?" they reply, "Nothing." I will tell you about what I was thinking. That I had just used my 'banking app' to complete a transaction, was on my mind. I began to imagine invisible money transfers flying through space all around me. I wondered what would happen if two different transactions collided in cyber-space. Would they cancel each other out? Could there be a mix up? This led to further daydreaming as I imagined my electronic transfer banging into Oprah's with the result that her bank account was transferred to me and mine to her. If you listen closely you can hear the imagined scream emanating from Chicago. In my reverie I mused about the things my family and friends would soon find beneath their chairs and the gizmos and gadgets my near unlimited resources would allow. The mere thought warms the very ventricles of my heart! If I were asked I would have replied that I was thinking about "Nothing." The idea is ludicrous and I would not like to admit this flight of fancy. Though I do not understand how these transfers actually work, I feel certain that there are protections in place to protect Oprah's fortune.

When Paul writes of God, in Ephesians 3:20 "...who is able to do immeasurably more than we ask or imagine", what is silly and hardly conceivable in the world of commercial banking is the very transaction God offers. Romans chapter four is all about God 'crediting' our account. That is putting into our 'banked' righteousness the rightness of Jesus and transferring all our unrighteousness to Jesus' account.

The Gospel of John records in John 19:20 Jesus crying out from the cross "It is finished." The word used in this instance is one used in financial transactions. It is like the 'Paid in Full' stamp at the bottom of a bill!

This is a transaction that is beyond my daytime imaginings! Only the mind of God could develop such a scenario. The cosmic transfer of my sin-debt to Jesus and all of His purity directed to my account is staggering.

How does one access this amazing offer? All that we need to do is to take a look at our own account and realise that we "fall short," and to turn in faith to God. At that moment, the electrons bang and the transfer occurs.

The greatest transfer happened not in a bank in Geneva but on a cruel cross on Calvary, where as Paul wrote in 2 Corinthians "God made Him who knew no sin to be sin for us, so that in Him we might become the righteousness of God."

The imaginary scream is not one of anguish from Chicago but instead it is the sinners.'

scream of joy, for a transaction so amazing that it is beyond any human daydream!

DAY 33

Persistence Produces
Romans 5: 3 - 5

I USED TO REGALE MY CHILDREN WITH STORIES OF MY FICTITIOUS Uncle Floyd. These were cautionary tales designed to teach the importance of persistence in pursuing our goals. Floyd was an almost brilliant inventor. His near expertise spanned vast areas but he always stopped just short of success. There is little doubt that we would have inherited millions from fictitious Uncle Floyd's estate had he been a bit more industrious.

In the world of cleaning supplies, Uncle Floyd created Formula 408, coming so close to the success of the man who picking up his research went on to develop Formula 409. This man cleaned up where Uncle Floyd messed up!

Fictitious Uncle Floyd was a melancholy man and this attribute did not aid him. He invented a dish soap "Kind of Happy." It went no where but again some one rebranded the idea and created "Joy" dish soap. Again, that person cleaned up.

At the time Marconi was first pondering radio, Uncle Floyd developed the AL/FL tuner.

When this did not work Marconi picked up the idea and persisted until the successful launch of AM/FM tuners. Today Marconi is a household name and no one has heard of fictitious Uncle Floyd.

In the area of adhesives Floyd gave up after his Northern England Tape did not stick. Others later picked up the idea and created Scotch Tape.

Other ideas of his were lubricant Dw-39, the personal listening device the Gpod, in fast foods "the moderate sized mac," and the list goes on. Floyd though brilliant, like so many in my lineage, lacked persistence and so the world never learned of his brilliance, until now. Failure is only failure if we fail to learn and grow.

The Bible has much to say about persistence. In Romans chapter five Paul tells us that "suffering produces perseverance." This is where Floyd failed. For him suffering produced mounting frustration and despair. He would quit just before the break through! I often tell people suffering through addiction that "It only has to work once." Each failure is one less one before ultimate success if we do not give up!

This kind of suffering produces something. Floyd did not produce anything memorable but suffering does. Paul goes on "Perseverance produces character." Character, true godly character is the stuff of successful living! This is the result of the sanctifying process God wants to lead each of us through. If we persist in our goal to follow Jesus then God promises we will become more and more like Him. This may take a long time which is why the stick-to-it attitude so absent in Floyd is so vital for us.

If we exercise perseverance God produces transformation in our lives and we realize a new hope and this kind of hope will never disappoint.

Fictitious Uncle Floyd's life was marked by disappointment and despair. We need not tread the path of this failed inventor but instead persist and put our hope in the God Whose express wish is to transform us to be like His Son.

DAY 34

That is Not Fair
Luke 10: 38 -42

I ALWAYS FELT SORRY FOR THE PARENTS OF THAT ANONYMOUS KID in some Third World country who would love my Brussels sprouts. Who did they refer their child to when confronted with the exclamation "It's not fair!"?

The complaint about fairness is a universal child go-to response and unfortunately it is rarely outgrown. In Luke 10:38-42 we read about Jesus' visit to the home of Mary and Martha. Mary is evidently enthralled with Jesus' teaching and sits at His feet to take it all in.

Martha is busy filling the 'good hostess' duties. She is frustrated with the 'unfairness' of the situation. She has been rushing about and her sister has been serenely lounging at Jesus feet! Finally, fed up with the situation she implores Jesus "Tell her to help me!" Jesus surprises Martha by demonstrating a lack of sympathy for the idea of fairness! Fairness is in fact opposed to Jesus' mission. Humanity without Jesus is careening toward the fate it deserves. The fair wages of sin (Romans 6:23) is death.

When I was a boy and complained to my dad about unfairness, he would shake a finger at me and say "The last thing you want in this life is to be treated as you deserve!" Jesus came not to bring fairness. He came in order that we might experience mercy and grace.

Mercy simply means 'not getting what we deserve.' Through mercy the demands for justice have been paid in full at the cross. I have earned no righteousness but in Christ mercy is extended to me. I am so glad I do not receive what I have earned through my selfishness and sin. I have continually fallen short of the mark, which is the very definition of sin! Grace simply means 'getting what we do not deserve.' The amazing grace of God is the gift of full and free abundant eternal life and all the other benefits of His passion. I am ever so grateful to benefit by the death and resurrection of Jesus and to be a joint heir in His Kingdom. (Romans 8:17)

Such 'unfairness' causes us to become lost in wonder and filled with praise! Dad was right! I do not want fairness, instead I am ever so thankful for the opposite of Fairness; mercy, and grace! Jesus' reply to Martha invites her to this same conclusion.

DAY 35

Golden Hemorrhoids
1 Samuel 5:1 – 8

YOU DO NOT SEE THIS ANYMORE, BUT WHEN I WAS YOUNG IT WAS not unusual for people to have a 'lucky rabbit's foot.' While it did not seem to work for the poor bunny it was considered a talisman of good fortune.

Though the Israelite army did not have a lucky rabbit foot they treated the Ark of the Covenant in much the same way. They thought that they could not lose if only they had the ark on the battlefield. Rather than consulting God and walking in His ways they relied on the Ark for victory. Superstition replaced faith and the Philistines conquered the Israelite army and captured the Ark.

It is in this context that a most bizarre story unfolded. The Philistines brought the captured Ark and set it in the tent of their god Dagon. Dagon was half man and half fish. In the morning Dagon would be found prostrate before the Ark. The Philistines would set things back in order and the next night Dagon again would fall prostate before the Ark. The Philistines began to realize they "had a tiger by the tail." Then things became even more dramatic. In the King James Bible, my Grandmother gave me, it says the Philistines were plagued with "emerods." More modern versions delicately say "tumors" but the more common word would be hemorrhoids. In the days before Preparation H this was a most inconvenient, embarrassing, and painful affliction.

The Philistines wisely decided to rid themselves of this Ark. They first sent it off to the Philistine city of Gath but the hemorrhoids followed. Eventually they decided they had to return it to Israel but they thought it best to appease the God of Israel by adding a gift to accompany the Ark so they made five golden hemorrhoids and five golden rats as a guilt offering.

The Israelites had sinned in trusting objects of religion rather than a dynamic relationship with God, with the consequence that the Ark itself was lost to them for a time. News of this led to the death of the Prophet Eli and the ultimate ascension of Samuel. Galatians 6:7 says "Do not be deceived: God is not mocked. A man reaps what he sows." There are consequences for sin, yet in Romans 8:28 we read "God causes everything to work together for the good..." The Ark was lost via sin but returned by the power of God and the visitation of hemorrhoids!

How uncomfortable must the Philistines have been! I do not know the value of five golden hemorrhoids but it was a more costly cure than a tube of ointment!

Israel presumed on past experiences but God, the Great I Am, is the God of the present. We are called to walk with him daily. There are consequences for our presumption. Let us feast each day on fresh manna. This may not prevent embarrassing ailments but modern pharmacies carry ointment today!

DAY 36

Lessons on the Prodigal
Luke 15:11 - 32

THE PARABLE OF THE PRODIGAL SON HAS INSPIRED MUCH literature and art over the years. It was also at the heart of one of my most memorable adventures. It was a hot sunny Manitoba morning when I received a phone call. On the other end was a pastor's wife from a church in Dauphin. She was planning a workshop for the fall and wondered if I would be available to 'open the Word' at the event. I inquired what kind of event it might be and learned that the topic was 'harmonics.' She explained that this involved the integration of mind and body. I was not sure what that meant nor what I could contribute. On the spur of the moment, I offered her what I sometimes have called "the evangelical 'No'" I said I would pray about it.

To tell the truth I then forgot all about it until I received another phone call just weeks before the scheduled workshop, looking for my answer. I was immediately stricken with guilt and I realized what a terrible position I would put this nice woman in, if I said "No." I replied that I should have returned her call and that I would be happy to come.

I learned that the workshop was about using our bodies through dance, and movement to worship God. She would be using Brian Doerksen's "Father's House" album as the venue. For the next week or so I immersed myself in this music and prepared my message. I did not want to go to a dance and movement event by myself so I invited my friend Aggie to come along. She has tremendous gifts in leading worship and I thought she might enjoy it.

When we arrived, I received an outline of the day. My preaching was to be later in the program but first all attendees were invited to improvise dance movement to tell the story of the Prodigal with Doerksen's song in the background. To say I have two left feet is to insult feet! I have successfully avoided public dancing for most of my adult life, but here I was paired up with my friend Aggie dancing out the story. I felt fortunate that the gym floor had lots of other pairs doing the same, so I would not be the focus. The hostess acted like a square dance caller telling us what emotions we were to convey. I had the part of the Prodigal and Aggie was to be the Loving Father. The instruction came for me to 'dance out rebellion!' I had not the slightest idea of how to accomplish this task.

In desperation I 'flipped' her off like a rage filled motorist. This 'dance move' struck Aggie as funny and she began to laugh uncontrollably. She did not want to make a spectacle of herself so she stifled any outward noises and covered her face as she shook with laughter. Her face turned red and tears began to roll down her cheeks.

One by one the other pairs stopped to witness Aggie as she seemed to powerfully connect with the broken heart of the Loving Father. We were the unexpected hit of the afternoon! This stands out as my sole moment of dancing triumph, if only it was real.

Later I felt that I was more 'in my wheelhouse' as I opened up the scriptures and taught about both sons consumed by selfishness. The younger says "give me!" and the older "you never gave me!" Both exhibit that same selfish sin filled attitude. The Prodigal though, changes his attitude. Now he says, "Father make me!"

All the while the Loving Father longs to forgive and restore. It is this change that God our Loving Heavenly Father longs for in all His children.

I let some time pass before I confessed to our hostess. She forgave me and called the day a 'wonderful success.

DAY 37

Hero to Zero and Back
1 Kings 19

SOMETIME BEFORE DISASTER STRIKES JACK AND ROSE STAND ON the prow of the Titanic and Jack proclaims, "I am the King of the World." This moment of elation however does not last. Soon he is shivering in the waters of the North Atlantic and sinking for the last time. This journey from elation to despair is not uncommon in life. When we are 'on the mountain top' there is but one way to go and the journey can be exceedingly swift!

As a child I remember that 'wascally wabbit' Bugs Bunny introducing Elmer Fudd to such a rapid descent with the words "Watch that first step, it's a doozy!" as poor Elmer once more plummeted to a typical cartoon splat.

Many of my favourite stories were of villains who appeared to have everything going their way, only to have the hero help reverse these fortunes. The hero gets the girl and the glory while the villain gets his comeuppance. It is the comic trek from the penthouse to the outhouse or jail house that so amused me.

Sometimes, though, heroes make this same trip. This is the test of their mettle. In this 'fiery furnace' they are forged into the instrument of justice that will ultimately triumph. Elijah took such a journey. He was literally and figuratively on top of the world after his victory over the Prophets of Baal on Mount

Carmel. He had demonstrated the power of God and vanquished these prophets of evil!

Just after his moment of greatest triumph Queen Jezabel declared a bounty on his head and swore that he would die. The man who had faced down hoards of evil prophets was suddenly beset with terror, at these threats. "Elijah was afraid and ran for his life." (1Kings 19:3) When he finally got around to praying it was not with the faith that he so boldly exercised on Mount Carmel. Instead, he prayed "Take my life."

He had gone quickly from the mountain top to utter despair. Fortunately, God attended to his heart rather than to his wishes. He gives the depressed Man of God a period of rest and rehabilitation. The strengthened Elijah goes on to complain to God that he is the only one left who serves The Living God. In a still small voice God communicates his plans which include Jehu as a new King and Elisha as a fellow prophet. God also announces that there is a powerful remnant of faithful Israelites numbering seven thousand.

Strengthened by the nourishment and encouraged that he is certainly not alone. Elijah picked up his prophet's mantle and returned to the struggle. That step from Carmel to the desert of despair was indeed a doozy, but it was not the end for the Man of God. His tale ends with a succession plan and a chariot ride to glory!

In 1 Corinthians 10:12 we read "So, if you think you are standing firm, be careful that you don't fall!" The mountain top can be a slippery slope as Elijah discovered. One of life's hard lessons is that only by being prayerful and careful can we navigate life successfully.

Watch that next step! It could be a doozy!

DAY 38

In Quietness
Psalm 46:10

I MUST ADMIT, I AM AN ODD DUCK. I REALLY ENJOY A GOOD silence. I grew up in a loud often noisy house. I used to love early mornings before the 'hub' and the 'bub' would begin. I would sit in the quiet with my imaginations and thoughts with great contentment.

Later in life I learned the value of silence as well. I learned that speaking my thoughts aloud did not always bring wide acclaim. In fact, expressing my ironic takes on events led to warmed bottoms and bloody noses. I eventually (I never claimed to be a quick learner.) glommed onto the concept of keeping 'my own counsel.' I still amuse myself with my thoughts but savour rather than spew them.

It is in silence that ideas come and are formed. More importantly it is in silence when my heart is quiet before God that He speaks. On occasion God has to increase the volume through trials and trouble to get my attention but I have learned that it is less painful to intentionally build time to be silent before Him.

In Psalm 46:10 we read "Be still and know that I am God." Jesus often went off alone to experience quiet communion with the Father. During these quiet times Jesus received direction for the day, His daily manna. In John 12:49 we hear Jesus say "...the

Father Who sent Me commanded Me to say all I have spoken." This quiet communion was the secret of His ministry and the source of His authority. In Matthew 28:16-20 Jesus delegates this same authority to all who would follow Him. It is direction and authority He realized through quiet time with the Father and we must access it the same way.

The 'World' loves noise and distraction. Distraction never leads to direction! The prophet Isaiah reminds us in chapter 30:15 "…in quietness and trust is your strength." Some days it takes real work to find stillness but it is the most effective work of the day! In this world perhaps God is asking you to be an odd duck. We can eider choose noise or the quietness that invites His presence.

In my quiet times I have discovered that God has a rich sense of humour. Sometimes He quacks me right up!

DAY 39

Everybody Loves a Good Mystery
Mark 4:11

HOW MANY MYSTERY WRITERS DOES IT TAKE TO CHANGE A LIGHT bulb? Two! One to insert the bulb and one to give it an unexpected twist.

Agatha Christie is said to have written several mystery novels in rapid succession. She finally stopped when her wrists began to ache. It turns out she was suffering Marple Tunnel Syndrome!

I began with the Hardy Boys and fell in deep like with mystery novels. I have read some brilliant novels and some less than well crafted attempts. A genuinely good novel may have an ending that is unexpected by the reader but when we trace back we see that all the clues were there. We have all the facts but we require the detective to reveal the mystery.

A bad mystery is one where the reader is not apprised of the necessary facts and has no means of arriving at the solution apart from the author telling us. Such writing is unfair and a waste of the reader's time!

The beauty of a good mystery is that the mystery can be known. It often takes a mind greater than our own, like Miss Marple, Hercule Poirot, or Sherlock Holmes to reveal it but a mystery is not mysteriously unknowable!

William Cowper wrote "God works in a mysterious way His wonders to perform." Too often we hear and read that as to understand that God's way is unknowable, but like our good novelists He reveals Himself and His ways so we can know Him. This does not mean we know it all for in 1 Corinthians 13:12 we read "For now we see only a reflection in a mirror; then we shall see face to face. Now I know in part; then I will know even as I am known."

Yet in His word God does reveal the mystery of the Gospel. Jesus tells His disciples in Mark 4:11 "The secret of the Kingdom of God has been given you." In Romans 16:25 we read "This message about Jesus Christ has revealed His plan for you Gentiles, a plan kept secret from the beginning."

One of God's most wonderful attributes is that He is the God who reveals himself. Apart from His self-revelation He would be unknowable. Like a good mystery novelist God has given all the information that we need to know Him.

In knowing Him we get to participate in writing a new story for ourselves. Apart from Him we come to a bad end but now we can live out a story with a glorious happy ending. I often thought about writing a mystery novel, but when it comes to putting pen to paper …

I do not have a clue!

DAY 40

The Mute Pastor
Luke 1:5 – 22

"I MUST NOT TALK IN CLASS. I MUST NOT TALK IN CLASS." I DO NOT know if teachers still make students write out lines, but mine sure did! I wrote so many lines that you would have thought my penmanship would be better than it is. I had a bad case of 'comic tourettes.' I would blurt out whatever funny thought that occurred to me. This was not always appreciated.

As I graduated Grade School, I was voted "Most Likely to Scientifically Prove 'Silence Is Not Golden.'" I was terrible at mathematics and inept with power tools so by default I made words my means of livelihood. I cannot imagine a life without words.

As I wrap up this forty-day journey with you, I am so grateful for the ability to communicate both verbally and through writing. I am grateful too for word processing devices so you do not have to strain to 'make out' my handwriting. What a set back it would be for me or any minister to lose these abilities.

In Luke chapter one we meet a priest (pastor) who does experience such a loss. Zecheriah was an old man. Fortune had not particularly smiled on him. He was childless, which in that culture was a terrible stigma, and he had yet to have an opportunity, as a priest, to offer incense at the altar. Finally, though it seemed his luck might be changing. The lot fell on him and he was chosen out of the thousands of Levitical Priests to perform this holy task.

While alone by the altar, suddenly Zecheriah was not alone! The Angel of the Lord appeared to him. This angel had a special message for Zecheriah. He was to be a father! Not just of any old child but of the one who would be the forerunner of the Messiah. Later in the chapter Mary receives a similar visit with prenatal news. She replies, "How can this be, since I am still a virgin?" (Luke 1:34) While she asked about the logistics Zecheriah's response was quite different. He replied, "How can I be sure of this?" Mary replied in faith and Zecheriah responded with unbelief.

We learn next that God takes unbelief quite seriously. Zecheriah is told that because of his initial unbelief he will be mute until the child is born. At first blush this seems like a humorous consequence for a mostly harmless error but for Zecheriah it would have been painful. He was a priest. Saying the prayers and blessing the people was his function, but more than that it was his identity.

Imagine your pastor or favourite television preacher being suddenly without voice for months on end! This is no mere slap on the wrist! First of all, when he emerges from the sanctuary Zecheriah was to bless the congregation. He had been waiting a lifetime for this opportunity and it would never come again. Because of his unbelief this honour was never to be his! For the next nine months he remained unable to publicly perform his ministry. He was left in lonely silence to contemplate the gravity of his unbelief.

Finally, the child arrives and the time to name him has come. Family and friends expect that the infant would be named after Zecheriah or his father or other honoured relative. Zecheriah calls for a tablet and writes in obedience to God's revelation "His name is John." This act of obedience brought to an end the nine long months of silence. Suddenly Zecheriah's unfettered tongue was loosed in praise and he prophesied regarding the magnitude of this baby's mission.

As our time sharing together draws to an end, let us take this opportunity to reflect on the seriousness and consequences of unbelief. God has made many precious promises. Let us hold them firmly! Let us doubt our doubts and believe our beliefs. Where we struggle perhaps we can pray a prayer modeled after this one in Mark 9:24 "I do believe; help me overcome my unbelief."

God grant us the gift of humour not to take ourselves too seriously but to always take you and your word most seriously, and all God's people said "Amen."

Printed in the United States
by Baker & Taylor Publisher Services